T0164787

Coffee Time with Daddy

My Road to Recovery

HARRIETTE PATRICK BARRON

WESTBOW
PRESS
A DIVISION OF THOMAS NELSON

Scripture taken from the King James Version of the Bible.

Scripture taken from the Holy Bible, New International Version®. Copyright © 1973, 1978, 1984, 2010 Biblica. Used by permission of Zondervan. All rights reserved.

The Author wrote from her own experiences and her Biblical perspective. The Author's views are not necessarily the views of Child Protective Services nor any Mental Health facility. The Texas Department of Family Protective Services can not be held liable for the Author's views on child abuse and neglect.

WestBow Press books may be ordered through booksellers or by contacting:

WestBow Press
A Division of Thomas Nelson
1663 Liberty Drive
Bloomington, IN 47403
www.westbowpress.com
1-(866) 928-1240

ISBN: 978-1-4497-2155-8 (sc)
ISBN: 978-1-4497-2156-5 (hc)
ISBN: 978-1-4497-2154-1 (e)

Library of Congress Control Number: 2011912318

Printed in the United States of America

WestBow Press rev. date: 09/06/2011

Contents

Acknowledgments

I want to thank my parents for all the love and support that they have given me. I want to thank my earthly father, Pastor William E. Patrick, who is now singing around the throne of God. He laid a good spiritual foundation for me in the beginning. He was a general in the army of the Lord.

I want to thank my mother, Pastor Hygeia Patrick, who is still fighting in the army of the Lord. Peace be unto you and all that you do. I love you because you have stood the test of time. If you had not prayed for me, I would be without hope. Thank you for allowing me to share some of your story, as well.

I want to thank my husband, Chris Barron, who is so handsome, smart and loving. May God bless you, my baby cakes.

I want the thank the late Sorita S. Without you, I would have never written this book.

I want to thank Jan Crouch (Trinity Broadcasting Network) and Bishop T. D. Jakes (the Potter's House, Dallas, Texas) for preaching sermons that loosened the shackles off my feet.

I want to thank all my friends and family for being supportive of all my writing dreams. Thank you all for encouraging me to write this book. God's people must be set free. We must live with hope and give hope to a dying and lost world.

I want to thank my extended family and church family. I want to thank Mary, Manassah, and William who were my support during my season of recovery. Thanks.

First Sip with Daddy

M ost of us have encountered at least one great person in our lifetimes, although we may not have realized how truly great he was at the time. I did not have an opportunity to personally meet Martin Luther King, Jr., Fredrick Douglass, or George Washington Carver. However, I did meet the greatest man I have ever known, my father. My father, or as I like to call him, Daddy, was a cheerful, wonderful, and positive man. He had a very creative personality and would often cook rainbow cakes for our birthdays. Daddy would often tell us stories of his exciting and mischievous childhood adventures. What a gigantic imagination and love for life he had. He would often retell my favorite story: When he was a child, his aunt Carrie told him to stop stealing unripe peaches off the family peach tree. Guess what? He stole the peaches, ate too many, and then his stomach had a terrible reaction. By the time Aunt Carrie made it home, my daddy's lips were swollen to double their normal size. When she asked what he had been into, he said, "Nothing." She laughed, as she could see the painful results of his having eaten too many peaches. His stomach had the worst reaction imaginable, and Daddy was painfully in the restroom for the rest of the evening. That was one time she did not punish him for stealing or lying because she figured he had been punished enough. There are so many stories Daddy told us about his triumphs and failures. He related that one of his biggest mistakes was dropping out of high school in his junior year. He always felt that he could have gone further in life if he had a high school diploma.

Daddy was a child caught in the middle of a bitter marital separation. He told me that he always hated to see good families split apart by violence or divorce. Daddy was the oldest of three children. He would go to school with a seemingly happy family intact but would come home to an empty home. From what he said, Grandmother would take her two younger children with her. She would leave him with his father. Oh, how he wept and felt totally abandoned. Why didn't she take him? Why did he feel unwanted and unloved by his mother? Of course his mother loved him, but he felt rejected at those times. He hated that she left him with his father, of all people! Grandfather was an ill-equipped caregiver. He drank alcohol and ran around with many loose women. Daddy was introduced to a new mother and aunt almost every week. When my father finally had the "sex talk" with me (of course, my sister had already told me about it), he told me that my grandfather would have sex in front of him in cars and hotels. Daddy expressed regret that he was exposed to sexual experiences at such a young age.

The most surprising story that Daddy told was about the time that he almost married his half sister! Grandfather was a lover of women in their small community in Arkansas. When Daddy was seventeen years old, he fell in love with one of the pretty neighborhood girls. They fell madly in love and planned to get married later that summer. Since there was not a father in the girl's home, Daddy asked the girl's mother for her daughter's hand in marriage. Actually, the girl had an unknown father, but it just so happened that the girl's father was also Daddy's father! The girl's mother had to tell her handsome, wide-eyed, and excited soon-to-be son-in-law that he could not marry her daughter. Oh, the pain those secrets caused. Daddy was shocked, hurt, devastated, and extremely angry upon confronting his father. After that experience, my father and the young woman never saw each other again. Daddy also told me that he was glad he never had sex with the young woman because he would have been even more devastated. When I heard that story, I made up my mind not to marry a neighborhood boy, just in case.

I admired the fact that my own father tried not to repeat the same mistakes as his father. He wanted to break the cycle of a divided home. Daddy told me that he was determined to do whatever it took to keep his family together. He spent quality time with his entire family. Both of my parents encouraged their children to reach their goals and dreams. I loved my daddy, and he was my hero.

Daddy was also a pastor, a teacher, and a powerful man of God who shared the Word of God with his children. He tried to be an example of a "real man."

At age six, I was taught to learn a Scripture in Psalms, the book of praise, which says, "O praise the LORD, all ye nations: praise him, all ye people. For his merciful kindness is great toward us: and the truth of the LORD endureth forever. Praise ye the LORD" (Psalm 117:1–2). Both of my parents instilled the Word of God in me at an early age. They would sit down with all four of us children and read the Bible. They made us recite the Holy Scripture and then demonstrate our understanding of what we read.

Far left, my brother, William, Middle Back, Myself,
Far Right, my sister, Mary, Front, my sister, Manassah

The Word of God tells parents to teach their children about God's word.

In most of this chapter, I am going to focus on fathers. However, my words can be applied to both genders. So many children are not fortunate enough to have a good father in their home. Not only did I have a good father, but I also had a godly father. My mother married a good and godly husband. There is a huge difference between a good man and a godly man. As Jesus Christ is the head of his body, so is the husband the head of his wife. God, directs husbands to love, nourish, and care for their wives, just as Christ cares for us. If you recall from reading the bible, Jesus Christ loved his body so much that he laid down his life for it.

It is effortless to relate to God as your Father if you have experienced the love of a good earthly father. If you did not have a good father, or were abused by your earthy father, then you may have more difficulty relating to God as your father. It is the plan of Satan to destroy your first perception of a father. You will be more likely to reject God as a loving heavenly Father if you did not have a good example of a good earthly father. Just imagine a minister saying, "God will be a father for you." You think, *I do not want a father! My father molested me! My father brutally raped or hurt me! My father mentally or physically beat me! My father cheated on and beat my mother! I hate my father!* Can you see that if Satan can ruin every concept you have had of a father, it may be harder to break your own rebellion and submit unto the will of your heavenly Father? What if you become a Christian and then have a male pastor? You will probably be angry the first time he gives you instructions that you do not want to receive. Your pastor is your spiritual father. He is called by God to give you instruction, discipline, motivation, and direction for your spiritual growth and development. You can count on it. If you did not have a strong, excellent father in your home, then watch for rebellion within yourself concerning your pastor. This same situation is mirrored with men who have a female pastor. If they had a problem with their mothers, then they will most likely have a problem with female authority figures.

God created the first family. He desired the husband and wife to raise their children together and raise them in the fear of the Lord. That was God's order then, and it is still his desire and purpose for today. God placed the husband to be the head of the wife, like Christ is the head of the church. The Bible does not say for women to submit to men, but it says that a woman should submit to *her own husband*. You follow your husband as he follows Christ Jesus. Ladies, if your husband is not following Christ, then he is following Satan. You do not have to submit to ungodly, unholy, and perverse ideas and desires from anyone. God is holy, and his actions are holy and right. Ladies, that does not mean that if your husband is not a Christian that he cannot tell you anything. If your husband gets off track, then you keep your eyes on Jesus and follow the Lord. Pray that God will deal with his heart and mind. Then he will be in a position to lead your family. In the meantime, you can still submit to the good things that your husband desires, but not the bad. If he is ungodly and what he desires is not pleasing to the Lord, then you do not submit unto that! Christ never abused, kicked, verbally abused, punched, or committed adultery on his bride, the church of Jesus Christ. Your husband should treat you like Christ treats his church. Yes, Christ rebukes us when we are wrong, but he has never abused his body.

The phrase "you made your bed now lie in it" is not in the Bible! Let's be clear: If God has joined your marriage together, then no person can break it apart. Some of these marriages were not joined together by God. We connect ourselves with people that God never intended us to be with. If you had to sneak off and get married or did not take your pastor's advice and married the person anyway or married someone your godly parents begged you not to or married someone who was already showing you signs that he was abusive, then you may have married the wrong person. God would never tell you to marry someone who is already married to someone else. People have blamed God for all kinds of things that he had nothing to do with. In some cases, God eventually intervened and saved the marriage, but if you were a victim of a divorce, don't blame God for not keeping it together. I am not saying that God will not give you grace to work it out, but he is never in favor of anyone dying at the hands of another. I have heard people say that they felt that God wanted them to stay in a bad marriage because he wanted to restore it. I am a witness that God can restore the worst marriages, and both partners can come out loving each other and completely restored through Christ.

If you feel that the Lord wants you stay in an abusive marriage, then stay. Have you ever thought of allowing the children to go to a safe place while you work things out? Children are often traumatized by witnessing their parents deal with domestic violence, alcohol abuse, drug addiction, or adultery. Their little eyes cannot handle seeing you go through the process of restoration. Sometimes it takes years for the other spouse to get off drugs, stop committing adultery, or stop abusing the other. If the spouse is abusing the children, then all bets are off, and the children must leave. You may be okay after the storm is over, but what about the damage done to the children? I am not advocating divorce, but when abuse is going on, you need to at least separate and get out of that situation. Keep in mind that it does take two people to make a marriage work. If you are married to an abuser or drug addict and he refuses to get help for himself and his family, then you have done your part. God will not join you with someone whose actions could kill you physically or spiritually. Get smart and get free before you wind up losing your life or your children. I have known a few women who have been killed because of domestic violence. The children were left motherless, and guess who the surviving parent was? The children were left with the abuser because their mom was dead! God is a good father, and he wants your children to have a good and godly father. He does not want your drug addict husband stealing your things, stealing your children's things, or bringing you back sexual diseases! How many sexual affairs does it take for you to realize that "this may not work out?" God is loving, and he would never ask you to stay with someone who is physically, emotionally, or spiritually trying to kill you! I am speaking of the husband that God intended for you to have and not the husband you may have chosen.

The father that God has chosen is instructed to be the head of the family and keep his children in order. God makes it plain that the family consists of husband, wife, and children. The husband submits to the Lord God as his leader and the rest of the family submits unto him as their leader.

Genesis 3:5–7: "When the woman saw that the fruit of the tree was good for food and pleasing to the eye, and also desirable for gaining wisdom, she took some and ate it. She also gave some to her husband, who was with her, and he ate it. Then the eyes of both of them were opened, and they realized they were naked; so they sewed fig leaves together and made coverings for themselves" (NIV).

In this Scripture, we see the first sign of disorder in the home. God placed Adam in charge of everything in the garden, including Eve. Here we see that after the serpent tempted Eve to eat of the forbidden fruit, she fed it to her husband, Adam. Adam heard God's direct command to take charge of everything in the garden, even the serpent. Adam knew that the Lord God gave him authority over the serpent and every other creature in the garden. It is doubtful that he would have disobeyed the commandment of God and listened to the serpent. Why else would the serpent set his target on Eve instead of Adam? Why didn't the serpent try to convince Adam that God was holding back information? Why didn't the serpent try to feed the fruit directly to Adam? Adam would not have taken the fruit from the serpent, but he would have taken it from his beautiful helpmate, Eve. The serpent knew that Adam would have put him in his place and used his authority over him. The serpent convinced Eve to take a bite of the forbidden fruit, and she did. Ladies, you know how we love to be involved in a good conversation. We love to talk to those who seem to understand us, even if it is a snake! Think about it. You know that man whom you wish you had never laid eyes on? He probably said "hello" first. The serpent's "hello" is what got Eve to listen. Obviously, the serpent did not scare Eve, or she would have run. He had to present himself as charming, calm, and intelligent. Ladies, that same serpent has been talking to us ever since. When you perceive that a snake is talking, you'd better start running in the other direction! You know, Eve talked to the serpent way too long. If you give the Enemy a few minutes of your time, it may take you years to recover from the effects of his conversation. The problem with men and women is that we usually don't know a snake is deadly until we have already been bitten. Only the blood of Jesus can cleanse and heal our snakebites!

Overall, husbands are still fighting to regain their rightful place in the home. *Submit means to defer to another's knowledge, judgment, or experience. It does not mean to be a doormat!* It basically means to let the other person have the last say in the matter. Ladies, stop giving your husbands a hard time over this issue. If we, as women, do not want to submit, then we should not get married. If you want to get married to a godly man, and he is telling you what is right, submit. He should not ask you to be a doormat, but just because the man makes a suggestion does not mean he is trying to control you! I know this is a daily task for most of us women, myself included. God put Adam in charge of everything, but when he laid down his rightful God-given authority, he never picked it up again. Not only was his family out of order, but also sin was introduced and the world went out of order. The world became so sickening and so evil that God had to destroy it with a flood.

Genesis 6:5–8: "And God saw that the wickedness of man was great in the earth, and that every imagination of the thoughts of his heart was only evil continually. And it repented the LORD that he had made man on the earth, and it grieved him at his heart. And the LORD said, I will destroy man whom I have created from the face of the earth; both man, and beast, and the creeping thing, and the fowls of the air; for it repenteth me that I have made them. But Noah found grace in the eyes of the LORD."

When Satan is in control, he will spread his devastation, darkness, sadness, perverseness, and all-out disorder wherever he is. Is your life out of order? Who is running your home? Is Satan the head of your home?

Ladies, if you marry a true Christian man, then he should be submitting to Christ as his head. However, if you as a Christian woman knowingly marry a non-Christian man, then don't expect him to be submitting unto God. You will have difficulty submitting unto him if he is not following Christ. If he is not submitting unto Christ, he is submitting unto Satan, to do Satan's will. God's Word forbids believers from marrying non-believers in Christ Jesus.

2 Corinthians 6:14–15: "Be ye not unequally yoked together with unbelievers: for what fellowship hath righteousness with unrighteousness? and what communion hath light with darkness?"

Imagine if a team of horses were pulling in two different directions; they would not get anywhere. You need to be going the same direction in order to be successful. If both you and your spouse started out as unbelievers in Christ, then you were not unequally yoked at first. Neither of you knew about God's way of living, which is different from knowing the Word of God and choosing to do your own will. Now that you are married, you have to wait and believe in God to save the soul of the unbeliever. Remain faithful to God, be a good example of a Christian, and pray for his salvation. Jesus Christ came to earth and set everything back in its rightful order. With Jesus Christ as the head of your life, your home and life can be restored back to God's authority.

The family flows smoothly when everyone is in his or her God-ordained place. Studies even show that children who come from a stable two-parent home are less likely to end up in prison or commit violent crimes. Studies show that young girls with stable fathers in the home are less likely to have premarital sex and become pregnant. Sons are less likely to join gangs when a strong father is in the home. Look at our world today: many of our children do not come from two parent homes, and we can all see the results. Christians, our homes are not only out of order, but our lives are also out of control. The world needs to see successful marriages in the church. It takes the power of the Lord God to heal our families and put them back in order.

I am not ignorant of the fact that some homes do not have strong fathers in them for one reason or another. Maybe there was a much-needed divorce, a death, or physical and emotional abuse—or maybe the man just left. These are just a few reasons for single-mother homes. Other women did not realize that the men they were with would not make good husbands until after they were already pregnant. Some women did not know Christ at the time and never found a man to marry. God is not ignorant of the reason that you are a single mother. He is well aware of why the father is absent from the home. In those cases, God will give the anointing and grace for leadership to the mother in the home. Do your best to make sure your sons and daughters have a good male role model somewhere in their lives. Fathers are desperately needed and wanted by all children. Use your pastor, male teachers, grandfathers, uncles, and good men in the community to supplement the absent father. No, it is not the same, but what else are you going to do? It is very hard to be a single mother, but it is much easier to lead with the Man on the inside of you. If Christ is the head of your life and your home, then there is a man in charge. It is The Lord God. He can give you wisdom on how to raise your children in the world.

Let's not forget about the godly fathers who have taken care of their children in the absence of a mother. There are terrible mothers who have abandoned their children in the middle of the night. Millions of fathers are left alone to raise their children for one reason or another. Some mothers became mentally unstable, some ran off with other men, and some just decided that they did not want to be mothers. God bless all you men who had to be both mother and father. The same advice goes to you, as well. Do your best to try to find great female substitutes to be role models for your daughters and your sons.

My father's first wife died of cancer at a very young age. He was left to raise his young children without a mother. When my older sister was very young, my father made an effort to comb her hair on several occasions. The outcome was terrible, but at least he gave it a good effort. My sister was glad that he finally married my mother, his second wife. She was finally rescued from the lopsided ponytail and nappy hair. My mother was a beautician, and my sister was glad about that. Daddy later admitted to me that he had made many mistakes in trying to raise his children alone. He unknowingly left them with babysitters who molested them, he punished some of them too severely, and he did not always let them have close contact with their extended family members. "If I could go back in time," he said, "I would change so many things, but I just didn't know!" He believed that fathers were important to God and to the world. Children need

fathers—or at least great male substitutes. Why is a baby's first word usually "Dadda"? Now you know why. God meant for children to have a dadda.

I remember seeing hot steam rising from my father's huge coffee mug. As usual, my eyes were wide and curious concerning anything new. Daddy seemed blissful while he blew on the steam. "Daddy, what are you drinking?" I asked. "I am drinking my morning coffee," he said. "Can I have some? It smells so good, but it looks ho-o-ot!" Although Daddy thought I was too young to drink coffee at seven years old, he gave me a sip anyway. My mother was not as thrilled when she found out, but it was too late. I liked it! Actually, I loved it! I drank coffee with my daddy almost every morning until I went off to senior college. Coffee time was our time to connect and talk about what was going on in our lives. He listened numerous times as I cried over many teenage boys. "Daddy, I was sure he was the one! Oh, I will never love again!" I cried between my tight braids, braces, crooked teeth, acne, and numerous broken hearts. I did all my crying over coffee. "The kids make fun of me at school! I am so ugly, and my skin is so dark!" Daddy listened over the years and, of course, he told me that I was beautiful and that I would fall in love many times over the years.

My parents headed our local church. I watched as they both opened and supported other small struggling churches. I noticed how their hearts broke as the membership dwindled for one reason or another. It seemed that they devoted so much love and time to help struggling souls. However, they would often receive so little when it was time for others to pour back into them. Daddy talked with me numerous times when he was discouraged. "I don't know if the church will make it this time, Shortcake. The people are just not responding to the Word. I don't know how long your mother and I can keep the doors open without financial support." Daddy had such hopes and desires for the small church they tried to pastor. He would talk about his ideas for building and enhancing his vision for the church. We both shared our dreams over coffee. It was our time to communicate heart-to-heart. Coffee time was our time to connect and breathe deeply over life. After coffee, we both felt ready to take on the world, and take on the world we did.

My Parents, Pastors William and Hygeia Patrick

My father was so proud of me on the day I officially graduated from college. I had overcome so many obstacles to graduate with a BA in sociology from Sam Houston State University. My parents cried and stood as my name was called from the stage. I was the baby in the family, and my parents had seen the last child through school. They would not have to drive three hours most weekends to check on me. They would not have to mail me money for food and clothes. My father would no longer have to move my belongings up three flights of stairs every year for the fall semester. We resumed our coffee time once I moved back home with my parents. I am glad that I came home that summer because my father had a sudden stroke two months later. My mother, my sisters, and myself had been at church having Saturday morning prayer. As usual, Daddy and I had shared coffee and spent quality time together. He was late due to his visiting the neighborhood church leaders early that morning. Soon after his arrival, he slumped over and dropped the papers that he had held in his hand. I noticed a bizarre look on his face but did not notice that he was ill. After prayer, we all went to the car and prepared to go home. Daddy looked at me but called me by my sister's name. He was handing me papers, but he seemed so confused. At first we all thought he was joking, as usual. I looked deep into my father's eyes, but I did not see him there. I knew, I felt, I discerned, and I sensed that something was terribly wrong.

My older sister drove Daddy home since he had driven his own van to the church. At home, Daddy sat in his favorite chair and looked at all of us in the room. He said, "Bring me my shirt! I need my shirt. There are words in my shirt!" We could not figure out what he was saying. Finally, he jumped up and went to get his Holy Bible off his bed. I had a choking feeling that I would never have coffee with Daddy again. Daddy was trying to ask for his Holy Bible. My sister and mother had previous nurse aide training, and they both discerned that he had suffered a stroke. His words were scrambled, and his eyes were blazing red. I gazed at Daddy trying to read a Scripture, but he could not get his words together. His spirit was still strong as he looked at us, trying to tell us that he was all right. After we took him to the hospital, he, my hero, caught an infection and died two weeks later. Daddy died with his hands raised as he praised the Lord. I always wondered how different people would respond at the last seconds of their lives. True Christians go to be with Jesus on that happy day. Those who have never accepted Jesus as their savior will go to a burning hell filled with torment and destruction. People can argue about the existence of heaven and hell, but people don't lie at the last seconds of their lives. They have nothing to lose. Daddy was a general in the army of the Lord, and he went out of this world unafraid and at peace. He went home to be with Jesus, but he left me the gift of our coffee time. I was deeply saddened upon losing my coffee buddy, but God told me that he would be my coffee buddy for the rest of my life.

After my father went home with Jesus, I began to set aside times that I could be alone. My mind seemed cluttered with the cares of life. I just felt a need to be quiet and those quiet times changed my life. As a Christian, you should have your quiet time with the Lord God. Your quiet time is just a time that you set aside to spend with the Lord in his presence, alone. Your cell phone is not ringing. You are not talking on the phone and cooking dinner at the same time. You are not yelling at your husband or children. Your quiet time should be exactly like it sounds, *quiet*. Today we live such hectic lives. We are always in a hurry and running here and there. We are picking up children, dropping off children, cooking dinner, making business calls, cleaning the home, working outside the home, and doing so many other tasks. It is no wonder that we often lose track of ourselves in the rat race of life. If we barely have time for ourselves, how in the world are we going to have time to spend with the Lord? I have the answer. If you can't make time to spend with yourself, more than likely you are not spending quiet time with the Lord.

Moms, you may have to steal quiet moments early in the morning before the children wake up for school. Night owls, you may have to find quiet time at the end of the evening or during the quiet hours of the early morning. Busy businesswomen, you may have to steal some of your lunchtime and use it for quiet time. Commuters, your quiet time may be while you are sitting in traffic. Christians, make time to spend quietly with the Lord! Can you pencil him into your calendar? Can you send him an e-mail every now and then? Can you call him on the phone (pray)? You can somehow find the time to do your other important daily tasks. Quiet time with the Lord is the most important daily task that you have. It takes work and time to maintain any relationship. You have to talk to co-workers, family members, your spouse, your children, and your friends. There is no way to maintain a positive and healthy relationship with anyone whom you do not talk to or spend quality time with. You must spend quality time with the

King of heaven for you to learn his voice, his actions, his ways, and his personality. The more you spend time with God, the more you become like him. People will say, "Hey, you look and act just like your daddy!"

I have the most wonderful times with the Lord while I am quietly drinking my coffee and reading my Bible. All of the Word of God is good. Sometimes it is so good that I holler out, "Preach, Isaiah" or "Lord, what did you say?" One time I yelled out, "Peter, I can't be mad at you, 'cause I denied him, too!" I love the Word of God, and I need it to survive in this life. The Lord reveals his secrets to me while I am reading his Word or praying quietly. That is our quiet time to discuss all things bothering me.

I still love to slowly savor every sip of hot coffee while meditating on the Word of God. I would not trade anything for my quiet time with the Lord. God drinks coffee with me and I love coffee! When I am sitting at the table with my Bible, it seems as if the Lord himself is sitting across the table talking with me. It reminds me of coffee time with my earthly father. Quiet time with my heavenly Father is priceless and essential. I think God's favorite coffee cream is hazelnut, or maybe it's vanilla or toffee nut. He also loves to go out to Starbucks every now and then. The Lord God is in me, and in a sense, when I drink coffee, so does he. When I hurt, he feels the intensity of my pain. When I grieve, his heart aches for me.

You may have quiet time in the bathtub, in the shower, or driving in your car. Wherever you invite the King of Kings, he will come and take a seat with you.

Vanilla Hazelnut Coffee

The Word of God is so awesome, and it is alive. Did you hear what I said? The Word of God is alive, and it breathes. When you really read the Word of God as it is meant to be read, you can feel yourself receiving strength. Your mind, emotions, heart, and spirit drink in the words off the page. The words are spirit and life. I have learned that the Word of God, or Holy Bible, is alive and that it feeds your soul. It changes your life. Jesus said, "It is the spirit that quickeneth; the flesh profiteth nothing: the words that I speak unto you, they are spirit, and they are life" (John 6:63). God's Word also says, "In the last day, that great day of the feast, Jesus stood and cried, saying, If any man thirst, let him come unto me, and drink. He that believeth on me, as the scripture hath said, out of his belly shall flow rivers of living water" (John 7:37).

I remember hearing the sound of my father brewing fresh coffee early in the morning. I could hear the steam rising off the coffeepot while it slowly percolated. Although the coffeepot was located in the kitchen, the fragrance would flow gently into every room in our home. The aroma, so strong and fresh, first woke my senses and then my body. Once I smelled it, I had to have a taste. The first sip of vanilla and hazelnut coffee was sweet and powerful to my taste buds. I savored every small sip and every deep swallow. I felt so much love in every sip of coffee because my daddy made it. Because he loved coffee, so did I. Reading the Holy Bible is like drinking hot, delicious coffee in a freezing cold, cruel world.

Sometimes life is so bland and mundane that we need something to wake up the taste buds. The Word of God will do for your spiritual taste buds what good coffee will do for your mouth. Just one taste of God's glory, one touch of his hand, or just one reading of his Word will change your life forever. The Word of God is *hmmm goooooood*!

Psalm 34:8: "O taste and see that the LORD is good: blessed is the man that trusteth in him."

The Word of God will change your worldview, rearrange your life, and conquer disorder. It gives you hope and life in a world of death and despair. The Word of God is like a body-sized mirror. You look at it, and it shows you your own reflection. When you look in the mirror, you look to see if your hair is properly in place and that your clothes are not wrinkled. When you engross yourself in God's Word, you begin to see yourself as you are. You see the good, the bad, and the ugly. Your own heart screams, "Uh oh, we have a lot of work to do!" People sometimes ask for advice about situations when they know the situations are wrong. "Can I have sex if I am in love with my boyfriend? We are getting married anyway." What does the

Bible say about sex before marriage? It says to flee youthful lusts. *Flee* means to run away—not to move in with lust. Some others may ask, "Is it okay if we live together before we get married? We are both Christians and we will not have sex before we get married." Why would you want to tempt yourself in that way? Would you invite a wolf to a rabbit's den? Most of us are not nearly as strong in our flesh as we think. You don't know what you would do in certain situations. You need to look at your decisions and present situation and say, "Let me line up with this Word."

My sister and I were in the marching band in high school. The drum major would often blow the whistle when it was time to line up. She would stand in front of us and mark the place where we needed to be. Since she was in charge, we lined up with the leader. After the football games, we would go back to the band hall and review our performance video. We all could see who was out of order and who was not watching the leader. By the time we finished practicing for the next performance, we knew our places. God is the drum major, and we all need to see which spot he has marked. He is yelling, "Get in line! It's time to get on the field." Wash your spiritual face with your Holy Bible. Eat the Word until your mouth burps out blessings instead of curses. The Word of God shows you the condition that your heart is truly in. Jesus tells us to love our enemies. If you hate your enemies, then you can see that you are out of line with God's Word. Read your Bible everyday until the words consume you. Let the Word of God change you from the inside out. You will become a living New Testament for the world to read. The Word will feed your weary mind and quench your parched, thirsty soul. It will fix your shattered heart and renew your broken spirit.

Before you pick up your Holy Bible, you must decide to believe that the Bible is God's absolute and perfect word to humanity. Although men wrote it, God inspired it. You must believe that the Holy Bible is the final authority and that every word is true. Do you believe that?

Do you believe that there are no errors, contradictions, or mistakes in God's Word? I have come to one conclusion. I know that the Scriptures have been copied many times over thousand of years. I know that it is possible that someone may have misquoted or used the wrong word while copying the original manuscript. However, in every translation of the Bible, the message of Jesus Christ is still the same. He was born of the Virgin Mary and died the death of all deaths on the cross of Calvary. Jesus died for the sins of the whole world. In every translation, Jesus conquered death, hell, and the grave. There is only one name by which all men can be saved and that name is Jesus Christ. In every translation, there is a magnificent heaven and a dreaded burning hell. No matter how many times it has been copied, the Word of God has all the keys that you need to experience a wonderful life on earth and eternal goodness in heaven. Please don't get distracted by the words of those unbelievers who say that they don't trust the Bible for different reasons. You can choose to argue about the Bible or go on and live up to it. Besides, obeying God's Word can only help you live a successful life. Those who are arguing over the validity of God's Word are steadily sinking into a burning hell.

2 Timothy 3:15–17: "And that from a child thou hast known the holy scriptures, which are able to make thee wise unto salvation through faith which is in Christ Jesus. All scripture is given by inspiration of God, and is profitable for doctrine, for reproof, for correction, for instruction in righteousness: That the man of God may be perfect, thoroughly furnished unto all good works."

Jesus was the Word in human form. Every word in the Holy Bible was wrapped up in the person of Jesus Christ. "In the beginning was the Word, and the Word was with God, and the Word was God. The same was in the beginning with God. All things were made by him; and without him was not any thing made that was made" (John 1:1).

He is God in the flesh, and he fulfilled every Scripture that came before him. When you read the Holy Bible, you are drinking, eating, tasting, touching, and learning at the feet of Jesus Christ himself. Where is your Holy Bible? Is it underneath your coffee table? Is it in the trunk of your car under your tools? Is it beside your bed? What have you done with Jesus? Do you remember where you left him last? The best place for the Word is in your heart, mind, and soul. If you believe in the Word of God, then you need to do what it tells you do.

Sometimes when I am reading my Bible I feel as if the words leap off the page and jump inside my heart. I am reading it with my natural eyes, but inside I am eating it. I am gulping all that it has to offer. I am consuming all the words and promises in this book of life. I realized that while I am consuming the Word of God, it is also consuming me. It will burn out unreasonable fears, jealousy, rage, depression, and all things unlike God. Just imagine that you just purchased your beautiful new gigantic dream home. On the outside, it is beautiful, and you are so excited that you can hardly contain yourself. Finally, with the keys in your hand, you open the door. To your surprise, you see fifty fat Texas-size possums, fifty fat cats, and a multitude of roaches residing in your home. What are you going to do? In East Texas, we would run inside, screaming like the house was on fire. If we did not have our shotgun close by, then we would grab a broom and start swinging. "Get out of here! This is my house!" You would see cats, roaches, and possums jumping out of windows, doors, and any opening for escape. Well, as you read the Word of God, it becomes alive and starts cleaning you from the inside out. Everything that is not like God starts jumping out of the doors and windows of your soul. Jesus Christ moves inside your heart, and sometimes he has to do a lot of cleaning and rearranging things in your life.

Hebrews 4:12–13: "For the word of God is quick, and powerful, and sharper than any two edged sword, piercing even to the dividing asunder of soul and spirit, and of the joints and marrow, and is a discerner of the thoughts and intents of the heart. Neither is there any creature that is not manifest in his sight: but all things are naked and opened unto the eyes of him with whom we have to do."

The Word comes in and says, "Fear, you got to go! Destruction, you have got to go! Get out of here!" Jesus is the Word, and he has purchased us with his own blood! Ladies and gentlemen, let's allow the Word to clean our house. You know, we all tend to think that we have settled our past painful issues. We tend to sweep pain and hurts under the rug of our hearts. The Word will clean us up and make us brand new inside! Ladies and gentlemen, the Word of God will consume Satan, the enemy of our souls. It will incinerate and destroy every barrier to your destiny in Christ Jesus.

Hebrews 12:28–29: "Wherefore we receiving a kingdom which cannot be moved, let us have grace, whereby we may serve God acceptably with reverence and godly fear: For our God is a consuming fire."

There are numerous places in the Bible when God fights with and for his people. God also sends his Holy Spirit onto warriors to win victories. God has always been involved with the affairs of his people.

God made man in his image and likeness. He formed man with his own hands and then breathed his breath directly into him. Men have many characteristics like the God who made them. Don't you have many characteristics like your birth parents? I have observed that men usually like to participate in a good fight every now and then. They are competitive by nature and will usually play sports or pay to see someone else play sports. Men love to see other strong men get roughed up, run over, tackled, dunked on, or wrestled to the ground. Men enjoy challenges, and they like to win. They love the smell and taste of victory. Even movies directed toward men seem to focus on aggressive behaviors, such as things blowing up, fast car chases, or someone fighting. For some reason, men tend to like competitive contact sports or some sort of fighting. I am not saying that is good or bad. Too much can definitely be a bad thing, but that is the way they are built.

It appears that God likes contact sports also, or maybe God just likes a good fight every now and then. He loves to terrorize the Devil and make him regret that he tried to overthrow God. I can hear God saying, "Satan, what do you think you are doing to my child? Do you dare try to stop my magnificent plan? You are interfering with my purpose for my child's life. You sent rape, molestation, fear, and torment to her as a child. Now she is having problems functioning as an adult. I called my child to be a light to the world of darkness—not to live in bondage to sin. So, Satan, do you want to fight with me?" Satan says, "Uh, God, I am hurting your child, not you. I am crushing her spirit, not yours." God says, "When you pick on my child, you are picking on me. I have already crushed you and ground you to powder. Now I will have to do it again. I am about to give you the whipping of your life."

2 Chronicles 20:15: "And he said, Hearken ye, all Judah, and ye inhabitants of Jerusalem, and thou king Jehoshaphat, Thus saith the LORD unto you, Be not afraid nor dismayed by reason of this great multitude; for the battle is not yours, but God's."

Nehemiah 4:20: "In what place therefore ye hear the sound of the trumpet, resort ye thither unto us: our God shall fight for us."

My father had a habit of rolling up his sleeves when he was about to give me a spanking. He would also roll up his sleeves when he was going to chop down trees or do a lot of physical activity. I knew that I was in trouble when I would see my father rolling up his sleeves.

My brothers and sisters, I sense that God is about to roll up his sleeves and fight for you. Fear and destruction, God is hunting you. Depression and abuse, God is coming to run you out of town. Spirits of harassment, God is coming to harass you. When God rolls up his sleeves, everything that torments, hinders, and destroys the lives and hope of his children has to go! It all has to bow down or get consumed by the wrath of the almighty God. When God comes in contact with whatever is bothering you, as we say in East Texas, "The fur is gonna fly!" God will fight with you, through you, and for you. I became very excited when I read about how God was going to cast Satan into the bottomless pit. I have already prayed that God would allow me to get a few punches in before he throws Satan over the edge! Right now we have to terrorize Satan through prayer, fasting, and bringing people from darkness to light.

Our God is skilled in the nature of spiritual warfare! He has hunted, tracked, and spied out the Enemy's camp. The Lord God has smelled where evil is hiding, and he has called out his angels to do warfare on your behalf. Only he knows the way that you can defeat Satan every time. No one can destroy God's purpose and plan for your life. You have the power to delay it, but it cannot be stopped.

I have known so many people who say they were called to preach the gospel of Jesus Christ, but they refused. I need to let you know that if God called you to preach, you will. You may preach on your deathbed, but you will preach. You may be preaching in hell, but you will preach. My mother told me the story of her uncle who was called to preach. He was a member of her church in Arkansas when she was a child. Her uncle ran around with loose women, drank alcohol, and decided not to totally surrender his life to Christ. The man even told others that he was called to preach but did not choose to do it. That same man was on his deathbed trying to preach to the nurses and all who would listen. Lying there, he continued to say, "Look at all that fire! We don't have much time. Everything is going to be burned up!" According to the reports, doctors and nurses tried to cool his body with ice and fans. His body refused to be cooled. He died gasping, clutching, and screaming about fire around his bed. The call of God is serious! God is telling us to get serious about his business. I imagine that the worst thing in hell will not be the searing, scorching, liquid, devouring fire. I don't think monstrous, hideous, howling, and tormenting evil demons will be the worst thing about hell. The worst thing about hell will be the horrific regret that lost souls will experience forever and ever. "Oh, if only I would have accepted the Lord into my heart! Why didn't I listen to the preacher? Why didn't I forgive those who hurt me? Oh, what mistakes I have made!" Can you imagine lost souls beating, pinching, and gouging themselves for all eternity?

Actually, it is an honor to be called by the King of heaven. He has called us to represent his kingdom here on earth as it is in heaven. We are the hands, feet, and mouth of the Lord God. If we open our mouths he will give us the words to say. If you can't think of anything else, begin telling others what God has done for you. The Lord told me to tell his people that whatever he called you to do, you must do it. The only question is where will you do it? I am determined to obey God and do whatever he has called me to do. He will give you the strength and resources to carry out his will for your life.

Jeremiah 1:5: "Before I formed thee in the belly I knew thee; and before thou camest forth out of the womb I sanctified thee, and I ordained thee a prophet unto the nations."

Matthew 22:13–15: "Then said the king to the servants, Bind him hand and foot, and take him away, and cast him into outer darkness, there shall be weeping and gnashing of teeth. For many are called, but few are chosen."

People are dying and going to a scorching, sizzling, and eternal burning hell every minute. I am glad my parents introduced me to Jesus! I am saved from an eternal burning hell because someone told me about Jesus. I believed that Jesus died for me, and I accepted Christ into my heart. Christians, sometimes we are afraid that people will reject us. We are afraid that people don't want to hear about Jesus. The truth is, some people do want to hear the good news and some don't want to hear the good news. So what? Tell them anyway. If you are extremely shy and can't seem to talk to others, then you need to find other ways to witness. Pass out gospel tracts or write it on a note. We all know the best way is to live for Christ in front of people, but sometimes you have to speak up. We need to do our part by telling the world about Jesus. God is the one who saves souls, but we are the ones who present the message of salvation to the world.

God has given us so many gifts and talents. I want to be found guilty of doing what I was born to do. Usually, whatever gift God has given you, that is where he will use you the most. If your baby tries to sing when you do, you may have a singer! If you see a child banging on pots and pans all the time, most likely he is a musician. My mother told me that I used to cry so loud until she would say, "I think that child is going to preach or sing!" My father said that when my older sister was little, she tried to boss him around before she could barely talk. Of course, she is still very bossy, but guess who keeps the family together?

If you are planted in a good Spirit-filled church, your pastor should be able to discern what God is calling you to do. You may have a feeling, a dream, or an intense desire to do something for God. Get in God's Word and find your place in it. Start by reading Isaiah 61. Do you like to help people? There is a great need for nurses, teachers, and caseworkers. You don't just have to use your gifts in church. The world needs you also. Do you love to minister in song? Are you an artist? Do you love to dance? There are so many ways to serve God with your gifts, but the main thing is that you are found trying to do what he has called you to do.

Ephesians 4:11–13: "And he gave some, apostles; and some, prophets; and some, evangelists; and some, pastors and teachers; For the perfecting of the saints, for the work of the ministry, for the edifying of the body of Christ: Till we all come in the unity of the faith, and of the knowledge of the Son of God, unto a perfect man, unto the measure of the stature of the fullness of Christ."

Christians, God needs all of us to spread his message here on earth. He needs us to tell the world that there is one King, and his name is Jesus. There is hope for the war on terror, and his name is Jesus. There is hope for our overcrowded prisons and failing school systems. There is healing for your sick mind and body, and his name is Jesus. Jesus is the only way to God and to his heaven. Jesus saves us! We need to let the world know that if they call on Jesus, he will answer. He always answers, but we may not always like his response. Our God is awesome, and he is alive and well. He has never lost any battle that he has fought.

By reading God's Word, we start gaining knowledge of how God uses men and women. We start seeing God's direction for our lives by reading his Word. When you read his Word, you get to know him. If you know him, you will not obey strange thoughts and worries when they come to your mind. You can say *that doesn't sound like God. God would never tell me to kill my children. He would never tell me to take my own life. He would never tell me to cut my wrists or overdose on pills. He would never tell me to blow up an abortion clinic.* God already commanded us not to kill. Murder is never justified. Self-defense can be justified. God gives life and hope, not death and hopelessness. He is the only hope for our dying world and for your destructive soul. Embrace the Lord God and all he has to offer. His arms are already open to receive you and all that you are. The great thing is that even when you make mistakes, God will be there to heal you and put you back on the right path.

John 10:27–28: "My sheep hear my voice, and I know them, and they follow me: And I give unto them eternal life; and they shall never perish, neither shall any man pluck them out of my hand."

Bitter Tears in My Cup of Coffee

My father and I drank coffee together until I went off to Senior College at Sam Houston State University. While away at college, my friends and I would talk, pray, and study over coffee. After the semester came to an end, I went back home to East Texas until summer school began. I enjoyed drinking coffee, laughing, and talking with daddy every morning. I usually attended summer school since starting college. In the summer of 1998, I prepared to go to summer school. I had no idea that many bitter tears would soon flow into my cup of coffee. One week before I was scheduled to leave for summer school, I had a very disturbing dream. In the dream, I was back at my college campus. I was trying desperately to get into the registrar's office, but the door was locked. I proceeded to the financial aid office, but the door was sealed. I was suddenly placed in a room surrounded by tall white locked doors. I tried to unlock the doors or find a way to shove my way through. I could not pass through the doors. I woke up puzzled concerning the meaning of the dream. Why would I have a dream about doors? What did doors have to do with my college campus? Why were the doors locked there? Once my eyes opened, I experienced an intense, suffocating feeling. I wondered if God was telling me not to go to summer school. Then I heard it clearly in my spirit, "You are not to go to summer school this time." It was clear to me that the tall white doors represented God blocking my path. The doors were locked because I was not expected to go through them. Job 19:8 says, "He has blocked my way so I cannot pass; he has shrouded my paths in darkness." It would be my senior year in college, and I was determined to finish along with my other classmates. I told my parents the dream, and they agreed that I should stay home for the summer. I told them that I had to go. I had to graduate on time. I did not want any further delays. I was anxious to get out of school and on with my life. I continued ignoring the warning of God and my parents, and I packed my bags and went back to school for the summer.

When I recall how hard I tried to go beyond the will and boundaries of my heavenly father and earthly parents, I still get a huge lump in my throat. The doors were closed because Satan had a huge ugly trap behind them. I can say that at that time, I did not know how important it was to follow the direction of the Holy Spirit. God tried to get a message to me, but I declined to listen to his voice.

Hebrews 3:15: "While it is said: Today, if you will hear His voice, do not harden your hearts as in the rebellion."

I was saved and filled with the Spirit of God, but I had ways that were not pleasing to God. I didn't think that I was being rebellious, because I thought that I knew what was best for myself. Like always, I thought I would be all right. My parents were both highly anointed pastors, and they always intervened when the Lord would show them situations concerning me.

They would lay hands, pray, and rebuke the Devil all the time, for me. I usually listened and relied on their hearing from God. I had never learned to follow the voice of God for myself. Your parents, pastor, people that attend your church, and your friends, are unable to answer to God for you. You have to answer the Lord God for yourself. He will ask you what you did. Only you can give account for your own works and your own soul.

Romans 14:12: "So then every one of us shall give account of himself to God."

It is good to be goal-oriented and to have a map for your life. The Bible encourages you to remain busy until the Lord returns. Be happy, get a career, marry, have children, and enjoy your life. However, what if your plans and God's plan are completely different?

Jeremiah 29:11: "For I know the thoughts that I think toward you, saith the Lord, thoughts of peace, and not of evil, to give you an expected end."

The only reason that God will interrupt your precious life plans is to replace your plans with his plans. Let's face it; sometimes we don't rely on God's plans because we are afraid that we will not get our way. Who do you trust? Is Jesus the Lord, the ruler of your life, or is he locked away in a tiny part of your heart?

That summer seemed to be the most scorching, sizzling, and muggy summer in all history. One could hear the brown grass crunch with every step. Heat strokes made the daily news almost every other day. It was very difficult for me to get admitted into summer school. For the first time, my financial aid was denied. I had great difficulty getting access to a dorm room. It seemed that every door of opportunity had been closed tightly in my face. I thought of going home and waiting until the fall, but I was determined to graduate on time. It was hard to admit that I wanted to go home, but my pride would not let me admit that I was wrong. I struggled spiritually and financially all summer.

Proverbs 14:12: "There is a way which seemed right unto a man, but the end thereof are the ways of death."

Final exams had been remarkably brutal, and I could feel the mental heaviness. My delicate C average hung in the balance. I had to pass each of my exams in order to graduate on time. Graduating on time took significance over all other summer activities. Soon I would graduate and move to Houston with my best girlfriend! We would both marry rich handsome men. I visualized being a world famous social worker, saving the world, and living a good life free of pain. I had my entire life mapped out, and up until that summer, it traveled on schedule. Because of my intense studying, my social life did not exist that summer.

Remembering the instant that I met him still causes me to cringe. Like a neglected baby outside in the freezing winter, I shudder at the thought of our first meeting. I sat in the student study hall the day he entered into my life. The nice, handsome stranger introduced himself to me. He appeared charming, well spoken, and demonstrated a deep, sincere kindness. The man introduced himself as Tony, and he began an intellectual conversation with me. We chatted about news, sports, family, and school. Tony mentioned that he remembered me from one year earlier. I had won Miss Mahogany 1997, and he had attended that evening. He noted that I was a beautiful and kind Christian girl. By the end of the conversation, it seemed as if we had known each other for years. We had chatted about two hours when he invited me to attend church and dinner with him later that evening. I hesitated, but he assured me that he only had the best intentions toward me. I agreed to ride with him since the church was only a few blocks away from the school. Neither of us called it a date; it was an outing to celebrate a new friendship. Since I did not make it a practice to let strangers know where I lived, I agreed to meet him at a mutual campus location. I thought that I was being safe and smart. I had a leading to call my mother and tell her of my encounter. Of course, she would have told me not to ride anywhere with a man I did not know. It is strange that we teach our children not to ride with strangers, and yet adults do it more often than we admit. Because I was late for class, I decided that I did not have time to call my mother. In reflection, Tony extracted more information from me than almost any one person ever had. Tony seemed a most interesting person, and we seemed to share multiple common interests. We went to an exciting church service where Tony had shaken hands with the pastor of the church and pretended to enjoy the service. We had enjoyed a pleasant dinner, a walk in the park, and an innocent conversation.

Even in my disobedience, the Lord still tried to protect me. As we walked in the park, a police officer pulled up in his car. The officer asked for both of our IDs. It was late, and the park had closed. Out of

the blue, the officer asked, "Young lady, are you here of your own free will?" Right then I felt no sense of danger. I felt safe with Tony. I assured the officer that I was not in trouble at the time. He gave me a long intense gaze and then told us to leave the park. Tony mentioned that he needed to purchase gas. He proceeded to drive us to a gas station, but the area seemed unfamiliar to me. As we chatted, Tony mentioned that he sensed someone would try to harm me. "Your smooth chocolate skin will drive someone insane and he may want to have sex with you," Tony said. He insisted on showing me self-defense moves that I could use on someone trying to hurt me. It still did not occur to me that anyone would want to hurt me, because I was a loving person and would not hurt anyone else. Until that point, safety had not been my concern. I felt utterly shocked as he said the words that made innocence escape forever. Tony told me that he was going to have sex with me. I told him several times that I would not have sex with him, but he told me that I had no choice in the matter. I cannot explain the feelings of urgency and danger that rushed upon me as my heart raced. My spirit said, *danger, danger, danger, get out of here, go, run, danger!* I insisted that Tony take me home, and he immediately pretended to agree. He drove me in the direction of my home but took a detour to a park by the airport. I saw the sign that said "airport this way." It was a long dark road and in an instant, I realized that I was lost. The car stopped, and I sat completely stunned and silent. My legs went numb, and I felt fear slowly crawl up my body. Like a helpless fly, I felt entangled in the powerful web of a spider. I was frozen and could not move. In a flash, I watched as Tony's face changed from charming to animalistic. I gazed as he removed his shoes and then strode casually to the trunk of his car. He ordered me to get out of the car. A large handgun was taken out of the trunk. He ordered me to walk with him toward the large field ahead. When we stopped walking, he placed the gun at the back of my head. Then, out of his mouth flowed the most horrible words of destruction. The words slithered off his tongue like a snake finally shedding his blistering spotted skin. Tony said that he was going to rape me, kill me, and then throw my body in a deep, dark ditch. My beautiful face would be unrecognizable, and no one would ever find my body. Oh, that dreadful park! Oh, that dreadful scorching summer evening. Although the sun appeared asleep, its heat waves seemed to dissolve all in its path. I realized that I was at a place of no return, and the events of that night were forever stamped on my mind. I tried to stay strong as so many things crossed my mind. "To fight or not to fight," had been the topic of many talk shows. I said I would only give up my precious body to God and my husband. At thirteen, I had taken a promise to remain a virgin until I married. I stood there hoping he would change his mind, but he was determined to destroy me.

I stood face-to-face with Tony; inside I heard the loud sounds of my will breaking. I stood there bargaining, stalling, and trying to appeal to his conscience. It finally hit me that I had kicked down every door that God had placed in my path. My dream came back to me! I had spiritually gone through the doors, and now I felt completely alone.

I then understood how Peter felt when he denied Christ after the third crow of the rooster. Peter remembered Jesus' words after Peter had failed the biggest test of his life. Before then, he had felt confident that he would never let the Lord down. He would stand for Christ under intense persecution. Peter was confident that he could handle any situation. Peter ran out and cried bitterly after he realized that he had denied the Lord. I did not deny the Lord, but I did remember his words to me while I was standing. Like Peter, I had felt confident in my own strength. Like Peter, I cried bitterly when I cracked under pressure. Like one who suddenly loses her eyesight on a busy interstate, without God ordering my steps, I did not know what to do.

Psalm 119:133: "Order my steps in thy word: and let not any iniquity have dominion over me."

Oh, Christian, we cannot make it on our own. Oh, sinner, where has Satan led you? Are you happy with Satan as your guide? Has Satan been kind and gentle with your hopes and dreams? Christian, you do not have the option to set God on a shelf while you go and fulfill your own desires. Disobedience has a penalty, and it could cost you your life. When you step out of the will of God, you open the door for an evil curse to come upon you. *The American Heritage College Dictionary*, third edition, defines of the word *curse* as "a cause of unhappiness or harm."

Deuteronomy 28:15: "However, if you do not obey the LORD your God and do not carefully follow all his commands and decrees I am giving you today, all these curses will come upon you and overtake you."

Oh, Christian, the Devil will not flee from you if you do not submit to God.

James 4:7: "Submit yourselves therefore to God. Resist the devil, and he will flee from you."

As Christians, we quote that Scripture all the time. The Devil will only run from you if you have submitted and continue to submit to God. If you are not under the covering of the Lord God, then the Enemy will stand there and mock you to your face. He does not have to flee from you, because you have no power. You have no power apart from your ultimate power source, the Lord God.

Tony said he would give me three minutes to make up my mind. He said my virginity was not worth dying for, but either way he was going to kill me. Confusion took control of my mind, knowing that soon my life would come to a sudden, violent end. Gazing at the stars, I felt as if every breath would be my last. Would death hurt? How long would I suffer pain? Standing there, I made my eternal peace with my God and his son, Jesus. Knowing that my soul would soon be in heaven with the Lord gave me some comfort. However, the warfare raged within my mind. I visualized how my sick mother would grieve my death. She would die after my disfigured body was found. Visualizing my father's enlarged heart exploding brought tears to my eyes. Then, as I felt the gun pressed harder into my scalp, I decided that I wanted to live.

2 Timothy 2:26: "And that they may recover themselves out of the snare of the devil, who are taken captive by him at his will."

That evening I learned that you will submit to being led by your will, God's will, or Satan's will. Only one can be in control at a time. If you are found out of the will of God, Satan can take you captive.

I said that I would comply with Tony's demand. I would have sex with him. He told me to strip slowly so that he could watch me. I felt that I was disrobing spiritually and naturally.

I can imagine that the serpent slobbered and slithered as he watched Eve in the garden day after day. He hunted, preyed, and lurked around her like a lion around a newborn calf. Eve went about her daily tasks feeling safe and secure. She had no idea that Satan was stalking her. He was obsessed while waiting for a chance to destroy the plan God had for her life. She did not know that anything was lurking with her destruction in mind. Most people don't know that the Enemy sets traps for them. You must listen to the voice of the Lord to avoid the trap of the Enemy.

I felt like Job when he said, "He has stripped me of my honor and removed the crown from my head" (Job 19:9). My honor was being stripped from me and my glory removed. Oh, when honor is removed, then shame moves in.

It seemed as if my soul began to strangle with every rough, painful glide of his hands over my body. I lay on the cold picnic table, gazing at the stars. Like a prisoner of a vicious war, I had been totally and utterly defeated. I had been stripped of all dignity, pride, and innocence. Feelings of kindness, trust, emotion, and love had been violently strangled to death by something called rape.

Would you believe that I heard the voice of God while I was being raped? Would you believe that I heard the voice of the Lord telling me that it was not his will that I go through this? I heard him say, "I am going to bring you out of this. Daughter, your sickness will not be unto death. You will not die by the hands of Satan." I know how hard that must be for you to believe. But I tell you, God was there, and he saw everything that happened. He did not stop the rape! Actually, God is the one who tried to get me to avoid the trap of the Enemy in the first place. Please do not think that I am blaming God or myself for being raped. However, I have reevaluated the events of that summer numerous times. In reflection, I did not value the voice of God or his protection. What I can tell you is there is a penalty for not listening to the voice of God. He tries so hard to protect us from harm, but sometimes we just are focused on what we want. Did the Lord God remove his hedge of protection surrounding me, or did I break past the hedge of the Lord? Tony held me captive for three hours after the rape. He talked to me and forced me to look in his eyes. He continued to tell me how the rape was my fault. I would not recover from this. I was too beautiful, I was too nice, and I should have agreed to have sex with him at first. Tony even mentioned how I started to call my mother but then did not. I had not revealed that to him, and I was stunned that he knew about earlier events.

Jesus told Peter that Satan desired to sift Peter as wheat, but Jesus said he had already prayed for him. Jesus was telling Peter that Peter was about to go through some challenging times but that he would make it out all right. Peter had no idea that he was about to be embarrassed and humiliated, betray his Lord, and break his own promises. It is funny how we all remember the word of the Lord after the thing has happened to us. I am learning to remember the Word of the Lord as soon as the situation approaches. Jesus still prays for us, just as he did with Peter. You see, we go through terrible situations in our lives, but because Jesus prays, we will not be destroyed. You may come out of the trial wounded, bruised, tearful, and dishonored! Christian, you will come out! God can and will restore you. You will then exchange your glory for God's glory. Baby, you can't bring yourself out of some situations, but God will move by his sovereign hand.

I could picture Jesus, my advocate, going to the Father, saying, "Harriette is your daughter; she loves you with all her heart. She has not yet learned the value of listening and following your voice. Father, Satan has desired to have her and end her life in a destructive and painful way. He has requested to end her life before your purpose can be completed in her life. Satan knows that her soul belongs to you, but he wants to end her life so that she will never reach the souls that you have assigned to her. Father, I come to you on behalf of Harriette. Please do not allow her to die at the hands of Satan. Father, I died for

Harriette. I died for all her blunders, shortcomings, desires, and sins. Now, Father, I pray that you will spare her life in this trial that she will soon go through." Christian, when God says you are coming out, you are coming out! No demon in hell can hold you when God commands your freedom. There is a time limit on every trial that you go through. God knows the time limit, and he knows that, with his help, you can outlast any trial that you go through.

When the Lord moves, at first it seems that things will get worse before they get better. The Devil knows God is coming to rescue his child. The Devil may try to hang on, but our God is a consuming fire. He will burn up every hindrance standing between you and him. Oh, Christian, nothing is greater than the power of God.

Psalm 124:7: "Our soul is escaped as a bird out of the snare of the fowlers: the snare is broken, and we are escaped."

When the Lord unlocks the door, run out of that situation as if your life depends on it. Your life just may depend on you moving when God says move or you standing still when God says stand still! Jesus told Peter that after he was strong enough, he would need to go back and strengthen his brothers. Isn't that just like Jesus? He tells you ahead of time that you will make it out. Don't let the trials of life destroy who you are and who you were designed to be. Allow the trials to make you stronger; you can choose to get bitter or better. I must admit, I was bitter for a long time. As I was being raped, I felt bitterness slowly crawling deep inside my stomach. Inside, my soul was strangling, kicking, fighting, and struggling to live. I felt my mind, my will, and my emotions dying inside me. God, Satan, and I were all in attendance that evening. In reflection, we were all aware that I was dying. Satan took delight as he saw me struggling to survive. God's heart was broken as he saw me dying. We were all present at the death of my will.

After the rape, I lay in an emotional heap of ashes. The event left me dishonored, dehumanized, and spiritually exposed. Tony did not physically kill me because he said that something had changed his mind. Then without notice, he put his gun back in his trunk, forced me back into his car, and then he dropped me off at my dorm room. I was dumbfounded as he drove directly in front of my dorm; I had never taken him there. Who gave him directions to my dorm? How did he know where I lived? How long had he known where I lived? "If you tell anyone what happened, you and your entire family will be killed," said Tony. After all, I had told him where I was from and some of my family history. I believed that he would kill my family and me.

Terrified and in great pain, I managed to have a friend drive me to the local emergency room. Upon entering the ER, I told the attendant that I needed to have a physical exam. She asked me why I would need a physical exam at 3 a.m. I stuttered and shook my head because I could not think of a reason. My hair was disheveled, clothing ripped, hands shaking, and there were visible handprints on my neck. It took her a few seconds to observe the tears in my eyes. She immediately admitted me to the hospital. I finally made my statement and repeated the events of the night, detail by detail, after she called the police.

Five hours after that first friendly "hello," I lay in the ER getting a gruesome rape exam. I felt like a legless man struggling to compete in a race with long-legged peers. The examining doctor noted that the rapist had left bruises and cuts inside my vaginal area. I overheard the doctors, nurses, and police talking about what a nice young lady I seemed to be. Having to give every detail over and over worsened my experience. With every new person I had to talk with, I began showing less and less emotion. My thoughts were, *What if I am pregnant? What if I have AIDS? How could this have happened to me?* Humiliation, shame, shock, and frozen emotions all plagued my mind as my body felt further dishonored by the exam. My innocent smile had been ripped from my face. For the first time in my life, I tasted bitterness. Like drinking sour lemon juice mixed with vinegar on a scorching hot day, that was how bitterness tasted to me. My healthy body showed bruises from head to toe. My lively dancing eyes now showed a blank, solid stare. Anger, despair, rage, helplessness, and hate filled my being, yet as soon as the emotions came, they escaped. I wanted to burst like a stick of timed dynamite, but the tears refused to come. The police and doctor had seen this before; they had met many young ladies in my predicament. They had lost count of how often it happened. That evening I became another female college rape statistic. Hours after the rape, I continued to feel Tony's cold and hurtful hands all over my body. After returning back to my dorm, I made an attempt to scrub away shame. "Guilt, I must rid myself of you. Humiliation, I must rid myself of you. Tony, I must scrub you out of out my mind." I scrubbed harder and harder until my skin began to bleed. My scalp felt sore as I tried to scrub the memory of his fingers from my scalp. Feeling clean, alive, and human seemed out of my reach. I was startled as I looked at my face in the mirror. To my horror, I saw a pair of evil eyes peering out at me. I did not recognize the eyes, but they were inside me. I knew that something evil had entered my body, and I knew that Tony had put it there. I heard the shrieking screams of demons inside my mind. Insanity tried to take control of me as the room spun around and around. Hours and days after the event, Tony's handprints continued to be visible on my skin.

The next conversation could not be avoided; I had to call my parents. Of course, they were on their way to pick me up from school. My parents did not say a word, but oh, how the sorrow filled their eyes. Since they came from a deliverance ministry, I knew they saw the evil that had entered their little girl. It was a long three-hour drive back to East Texas. I could hear screams inside my head for the entire three hours. My eyes were not consumed with tears, but they were piercingly ice-cold. My eyes were void of warmth and compassion. Rage filled my eyes, and so much pain filled my heart. My heart was shattered in a million pieces. My hopes and dreams were destroyed before my eyes. I knew that eventually I would need a spiritual heart transplant. Silently, I began to pray for myself: *Lord, I am in trouble. Please help me.* Although I returned home confused and bitter, my father and I resumed our coffee time. However, instead of a lively conversation, I sat crying bitter tears into my cup of coffee. Daddy didn't know what else to do except love me and allow the tears to fall. In the past, I had cried over teenage issues, but had never experienced anything so painful to my spirit. Soon after returning home, my mother took me to a small ladies prayer meeting. She told the ladies what happened, and they began to pray for me..They were so gentle, so loving, but they were aggressive with the evil spirits inside my mind. Since something evil had entered my body, it had to be cast out. Out of my mouth flowed piercing screams of anguish. Oh, the pain inside my heart. I felt relief after the prayer meeting, and my cold, blank stare was now warm and tender. I cried and cried until there were no more tears. My eyes had swollen, but at least now I could get some sleep.

Corinthians 6:16: "What? Know ye not that he which is joined to a harlot is one body? for two, saith he, shall be one flesh."

Whether by choice or force, once two people have sex, they are bound within their souls. In biblical times, once a man had sex with a woman, she was officially his wife. They had made a blood covenant, and they were married.

Whatever spirit is in that other person, it steps inside your mind, will, and emotions. You become linked in your soul as if you were tied

with a strong rope or cord. Soul ties have to be broken by the power of the Holy Spirit. Spirits cannot be talked out, cried out, counseled out; they must be cast out in Jesus' name. Mark 10:8 says, "and the two will become one flesh. So they are no longer two, but one." You become one with that person; it doesn't matter if it was by choice or force. That is why intimacy is only for marriage, and close bonds are only to be formed with those of the same spirit—the spirit of God or of Satan. However, because of the world we live in, sometimes a child's virtue is ruined at an early age. Victims are both male and female. Satan has no preference as to who he tries to destroy. Sometimes the victim never had a chance to choose intimacy with a mate because someone took that decision away. Other people who did not know the Lord may have had many sexual partners and formed bonds with them. They had no idea that their sexual partners would be tied to them for the rest of their lives.

Let's even go further. Soul ties can be formed by molestation, traumatic experiences, or even close relationships between two people. Why do you think some young people take on the personalities of their friends? A good Christian boy will suddenly find himself stealing, lying, cheating, and even dressing like his ungodly friends. Have you ever found yourself acting like someone else? 1 Corinthians 15:33 says, "Be not deceived: evil communications corrupt good manners." When you open up your heart to people, you form a soul tie with them and the spirit in them transfers to you.

Yes, I had a right to be angry after what happened to me, but the rage inside was not natural. I felt an urge to hate, kill, and destroy everything male. I had formed an unholy soul tie with the man who raped me, and the screams I heard inside me were his demons. His demons entered my mind and body at the time of the rape. However, I wanted to be free, and I wanted everything in me that was not like God to come out. I refused to be a house for any unclean spirit. I am glad there were prayer warriors around me to cast those spirits out, and I was more than willing to let them go. I must admit that they did not all go at one time. Unknown to me, I had several demons of my own that were already there. I had mental trauma that I did not know was there. I had three soul ties from previous molestations during my childhood. I would get more deliverance as the Holy Spirit revealed more of these issues.

Later I will lead you through a prayer for breaking soul ties with those you have formed a bond with. You can be free in Jesus' name. You don't have to carry those painful memories, spirits, and emotional ties from those who have hurt you. No matter how old you are, if you have never broken the soul ties with those you have formed bonds with, their spirits are still inside you. Why do you think a lot of married women have problems with sex years after they have been victimized? The problem keeps resurfacing because the soul tie was never broken with the perpetrator. The perpetrator is still a part of your life because he or she is still in you. My deliverance happened in layers because I had more to deal with than I thought. Your deliverance from some things may take longer than someone else's deliverance. I was delivered in a process, and it took years, but God gave me the strength to deal with one issue at a time. Our God is patient, and he knows what you can handle. Most likely, if you have been through a lot of trauma, it may take longer for you to heal. If much pain is given, then much healing is required. Let the Lord take you through every stage of healing and deliverance that you need to go through. You may have traumatic memories that you have blocked away. When the Lord brings one of these memories up, that means it is time for you to deal with it. You may not be able to do it alone. Get spiritual counseling if you need to, but whatever you do, deal with it so that you can deal with the next issue on the list. Don't rush the process; remember the Lord God is with you. He has given you an entire lifetime to deal with your inner struggles.

Imagine that you are in elementary school. You get certificates for every subject that you master from the first grade until you graduate from the twelfth grade. Some students fail because they did not learn what they were supposed to learn. Students gain experience and knowledge every time they pass a test. We are all in school here on earth. Sometimes we keep going through the same situations until we pass the test and move on. The Lord wants us to gain wisdom and enlightenment from every experience that we go through. Listen, we live in a world of people, and we are bound to collide with each other. People will hurt us, people will offend us, people will use us, and people will make mistakes without intending to cause us harm. People make mistakes and sometimes we, the bystanders, get caught up in their madness. God is faithful! As long as you have Christ as the head of your life, he will always bring you back to where he wants you to be. Honestly, most of us have taken detours in life. We have taken our own roads and been wise in our own eyes. We have all failed God at one time or another. The good news is that when we fall, God will pick us up! He is not surprised by anything that you do or any mistake that you make. He has already arranged for your healing and deliverance. Why did God put the gift of healing in a doctor's hand? He knew people would become ill. Why did God put the ability to fix cars in a mechanic's hand? He knew people's cars would break down. Why did God give preachers the ability to ignite your soul through the spoken word? God knew that you would need encouragement and guidance.

When I was seven years old, my mother bought me the most beautiful doll for Christmas. I loved the doll and played with it all the time. I cradled it, cuddled it, slept with it, and pretended to feed and nourish it. She had on blue silk from head to toe. One day, I accidentally tore off her arm and did not know how to get it back on. I went to my mother, crying, begging, and heartbroken. My favorite doll was broken, and I could not fix it! The first thing my mother did was look on the tag to see who made the doll. She knew that the creator of the doll was the best person to sew the arm back on. However, she carefully examined the doll and decided that she was able to sew the arm back on herself.

Sometimes we are broken and almost destroyed by the trials of this life. We believe that life is unfair. The truth is, life is unfair, but we still have to live it, breathe it, and function in it. We need to say, "God, I am broken, and only you know how to truly fix me. Others have torn me apart, but some have unsuccessfully tried to put me back together."

You need to go back to the Creator of your mind, body, and soul! Take all your wounds, anguish, guilt, and shame to the manufacturer. We must have Jesus in our hearts so that we can survive, heal, and make it in this jungle that we call life. The Lord God will even lead you around certain situations. He is our compass and flashlight in a world of misdirection and extreme darkness. He knows what you can and cannot handle. Listen to the voice of the Lord, and he will help you avoid so many situations.

Believe me, I know that there are some things that it may take you years to recover from. It is sad to see a bitter, crippling, and mean elderly person. I have known people who were in nursing homes and were bitter, cursing, and filled with anger. They were angry and lashed out at everyone trying to help them. You can bet that they were hurt or made angry years earlier and that they never forgave those who caused them pain. People, we must forgive. Forgiveness frees you, and it gives God permission to deal with the other person. When you don't forgive, you hold the other person in your heart and feast on his memory. Let him go! You can ask the Lord to forgive him through you. Take one step at a time and deal with one issue at a time.

Go ahead, sit and make your list of things you need to do. Then get out your Bible and find everything concerning your problem in the Word of God. God's Word will tell you how to deal with bitterness, rage, unforgiveness, and all things bothering you. Pray earnestly for God to help you through your healing process. Remember, God is the Creator, and if you are broken, no one can fix you like he can. Since he made you, he knows what you need to be victorious in your life's journey. Let's go back to the Creator of all things, the Lord God.

Breaking Soul Ties—A Prayer Given to me by the Holy Spirit

Father God, in the name of Jesus, I thank you for creating me to love and to serve you. Lord, I ask you to forgive me for all my sins and all that I've done wrong. Father, forgive me for the sins I've committed knowingly and unknowingly. Father, I am in covenant with someone who has hurt me. I have a soul tie with _____ (if you can remember the name or names). Father, whether our soul tie was forcefully or willingly made, I ask you to break and destroy it in Jesus' name. Lord, I break the soul tie with _____ (insert name or names), and Lord, replace that severed tie between _____ and me with a soul tie between you and me. Father, I rededicate my mind, will, and emotions to you. Lord, heal every broken and cracked place in my mind, will, and emotions. Father, in Jesus' name, I dethrone every unclean spirit that sits on the throne where Jesus is to be seated. I dethrone molestation, pity, self-destruction, shame, guilt, suicide, death, and self-hatred in the name of Jesus. Lord Jesus, take your place on the throne of my heart. I dethrone selfishness, lust, perversion, lack, poverty, and fear of the unknown in Jesus' name. I dismantle every weapon that has been raised against me by the Enemy. Father, I ask you to destroy every plan and assignment of the Enemy. Lord, establish your plan in my life. Oh, God, take your place on the throne in my home and my life. Oh, Lord Jesus, I recognize you as the absolute head of my life. You are the head, and I am part of your body. I choose to forgive everyone who has hurt me and desired to bring my life to an end. I forgive _____ (insert name or names) in the person of Jesus Christ. Lord, I choose to forgive him/her/them because you have forgiven me. You are the judge of all flesh, and I turn every hurt over to you. Lord, I reconnect my will with your will. Let this mind be in me which was also in Christ Jesus. In Jesus' name, I pray. Amen.

Now you are on your way to a marvelous recovery in Jesus' name.

My Journey of Healing Begins

When you go through a tragedy, you mourn and you grieve. Grieving is part of the process of healing. I did not know that I was grieving, but I was. After the rape, I felt as if someone very close to me had suddenly died. Someone did die, and it was the person I had been. In a sense, my will, my emotions, and my dreams had been killed by something called rape. I could feel someone inside me strangling, kicking, and struggling to live. I wanted to live, but by the end of the rape, something in me had suffocated to death.

Ezekiel 16:6–7, "Then I passed by and saw you kicking about in your blood, and as you lay there in your blood I said to you, 'Live!' I made you grow like a plant of the field. You grew up and developed and became the most beautiful of jewels. Your breasts were formed and your hair grew, you who were naked and bare" (NIV).

This Scripture refers to the Lord God seeing his people, Israel, struggling in life. Imagine an awful person forcing her way into a hospital delivery room. She snatches the baby as soon as it is delivered. It doesn't matter to her that the navel cord is not yet cut or that fluid is still on the baby or that the baby's eyes are still closed. While running out of town, she hatefully throws the baby into a field of thorns and rocks. A caring man passes by and sees a baby girl strangling, kicking, and drowning in her own blood.

With compassion, he picks up the baby and cleans her off with his own clothing. He loves her, nourishes her, and raises her as his own beautiful daughter. I felt that I was that baby who had been thrown into a ditch to die. According to the Bible, all life is in the blood. God saw me polluted in my own life. I was kicking and drowning under depression, anxiety, rage, and despair. He said unto me, "Live," and I did. I was not the same person. Now I just needed to know who I was.

Having to leave school, feeling mentally unstable, and suffering through nightmares and severe depression caused me to develop a complete hatred for myself. The rest of the year, I proceeded to purposely gain fifty pounds. I desired to make myself so unattractive that no man would ever desire to look at me again. I could not smile, and I refused to wear makeup or any fitted clothing. I began pinching myself because I hated the sight of my own skin. Trying to conceal my spiritual untreated wound was painful. Craving to hide from view, I stayed beyond the reach of everyone. I would like to tell you that my season of pain was soon forgotten. I would love to tell you that God immediately healed my wounded heart and restored my soul. I would like to tell you that I was back to normal in no time, but that is not what happened.

Psalm 6:6: "I am weary with my groaning; all the night makes my bed to swim; I water my couch with my tears."

It took me at least three years to completely heal from the rape. What I can tell you is that God was faithful, and he walked me through every emotion of rage, bitterness, loneliness, and humiliation. There were times when my heart felt so broken that I literally could not speak. For the first year, I suffered relentless, painful nightmares. I would relive the rape over and over. I would have visions in the daytime of the events. I would have huge bags under my eyes daily due to my lack of sleep. It seemed that at midnight warm tears would stream down my face and then the nightmare would follow. When the night would approach, evil spirits would torment me. It seemed as if large black cats would come in my room to smother me. I could not breathe! I kicked, I shook, and I wailed, and then I would wake up screaming.

My earthly father was very sweet during my season of pain. He would come in my room and sit with me every night. He would listen as I talked and cried. I told him my dreams and my nightmares. Daddy would pray for me, and he did all that he could to keep from crying in front of me. Oh, the pain that I felt as I sunk lower and lower into depression. There are some trials that you will go through alone. There are some places where others, aside from God, cannot go. Momma could not cure me. Daddy could not repair me. The counselor could not piece me back together. My wound was invisible and deep. My life was so destroyed that only the sovereign hand of a Holy God could reach deep down and pull up the pain. He removes burdens and destroys yokes of bondage.

Isaiah 26:28: "And it shall come to pass in that day, that his burden shall be taken away from off thy shoulder, and his yoke from off thy neck, and the yoke shall be destroyed because of the anointing."

I woke up crying because every time I closed my eyes, I saw Tony. Every time I took a shower, I felt his hands all over my body. I wailed in the night because I felt that I had let God and my family down. Tears flowed because my life's dreams seemed so far out of my reach. I moaned because no one could speed up my recovery. I screamed because I wanted to be free and whole. I yelled because I was shattered in a million pieces. I felt like Blind Bartemus in the Bible, sitting by the roadside begging. It is unknown how long this blind man had sat there begging and feeling sorry for himself. He had sat there waiting for people to help him, and he depended on them for his survival. One day he heard that Jesus was passing by, and he yelled out, "Jesus, Son of David, have mercy on me!" (Luke 18:38

NIV). I felt that I was spiritually blind and depended on someone to come and help me survive. Out of my soul, I cried, "Jesus, have mercy on me. Jesus, I did not listen when you tried to protect me. Lord, I need your mercy, because I am alone in this garden. I am alone in this wilderness. Jesus, Son of David, have mercy on me. Have mercy on who I was trying to be. Have mercy on who I am struggling to be. Deliver me from all evil." Out of desperation I cried, "Lord, heal my broken heart, because only you can!"

One time I attempted to pray, but I could no longer speak words out of my lips. The only thing I could do was cry. I heard the Lord say, "No need to talk; your tears are coming up to me as words." Oh, what comfort I felt. Now I realize that when your heart is so broken that words cannot pass your lips, God still hears your heart's cry.

Psalm 61:1–2: "Hear my cry, O God; attend unto my prayer. From the end of the earth will I cry unto thee, when my heart is overwhelmed: lead me to the rock that is higher than I."

You see, the hurt was stronger than I, but God was stronger than it! God is higher, stronger, and superior to any problem. The Lord God is a shelter in the storms of life. You have to swiftly run to him, because there is no greater help on earth. Oh, the broken hearts of God's people. I have good news! None of your tears have been wasted.

Psalm 56:8: "Thou tellest my wanderings: put thou my tears into thy bottle: are they not in thy book?"

Did you hear that? I don't care if you cried and no human eye saw your tears. I don't care if you were humiliated and no one saw your pain. If you wanted to cry, but the wrath inside you would not allow it, God saw your heart's cry. Your tears cry out for justice. Your tears cry out for mercy. Your tears cry for every trauma you have suffered. When you can't speak, your tears are screaming loudly, "Lord, do something about it!" Every sigh that flows painfully out of your mouth comes up as words in heaven's throne room. Every painful breath of a suffering soul screams loudly. He says, "I heard that!"

Psalm 34:18: "The LORD is close to the brokenhearted and saves those who are crushed in spirit."

God saw, and he knows what happened. Just the fact that God knows gives me comfort. Even if God does not immediately intervene in your situation, take comfort in knowing that he knows. As it has been said before, "if God doesn't deliver us, we know he is able!" Since God knows about it, he will do something about it! You may not see him take care of the situation. I promise you this: when you call out to God, he will help you.

2 Kings 20:4–6: "Turn again, and tell Hezekiah the captain of my people, Thus saith the LORD, the God of David thy father, I have heard thy prayer, I have seen thy tears: behold, I will heal thee."

I Need A Whole Pot of Coffee

Within one pot of coffee lie several cups of coffee. Usually there are twelve cups of coffee in one pot. In times of stress, I usually drink more coffee than normal because it helps me relax. As I have said, my private time entails drinking a cup of coffee while talking to the Lord, but I can recall a time when I didn't need one cup—I needed a whole pot! I needed to spend more time with him than usual. I needed God more than I ever had before.

As a Christian, you should walk closely with the Lord! During times of crisis, you must rely more heavily on him for every breath. How can someone live a happy and victorious life after he has experienced a hideous catastrophe? I know several of you may have been through terrible, even unmentionable, situations. Let's be honest: your recovery will not be easy, but it is necessary. You have to recover, or you will go down into a pit for the rest of your life. Say it to

yourself: "I have to recover! Staying in this pit is not an option. I want to get out! I have to get out." Hey, you are not so low down that the Lord cannot reach down and pick you up.

Isaiah 59:1: "Surely the arm of the LORD is not too short to save, nor his ear too dull to hear."

You may have layers upon layers to work through. Usually, you are the first one to know if you are a mess. You may be the last one to actually admit it. Run to God in hard times. Don't run from him. He is your help. There are many people who can't handle the internal pain. They run to drugs, sex, homosexuality, lesbianism, alcohol, and other people. The problem may be too painful to even discuss with themselves, let alone anyone else. I have discovered that problems, secrets, and silent pain all refuse to be ignored. They show themselves one way or another. I also have discovered that a lot of sins that people commit are actually  rooted in pain and trauma. There is a cause for every problem. Why are you so quick to get angry? Why don't you trust anyone? Why are you so bitter toward men or women? There is a source and a root to your issues. The painful part is discovering what started the issue or, better yet, who started the issue. Everything except God has a beginning. Some people do anything not to face the pain hidden deep within the soul. They will do anything to drown out the loudly screaming, pained voices from the past. They will do anything to drown out the nightmares that haunt them at night.

I still remember when the Lord God challenged me to give him all my pain. It was six months after the rape, and I was mentally tormented. I appeared tired, sad, bitter, and angry all the time. I seemed very troubled, and my pastor called me up for prayer. As a matter of fact, whenever I would go to other churches, the speaker would call me out and minister healing to me. These speakers did not know me, but God did. That morning, the pastor laid hands on me. I heard a resounding voice say, "Let me have it!" I knew it was the voice of the Lord, and I knew exactly what he was talking about. I also heard my spirit say, "Lord, it is too painful to open that door. I just want to forget it!" Standing there, I could feel the war rage inside me. I did not want to give my pain to God, because he would have to dig too deep. I was afraid of what he would find and what he would reveal. I don't know how long I stood there, but it seemed like an eternity. Standing there in front of the altar, I decided to let God take control and begin the healing. God can heal it, but you need to reveal it. I stood there, presenting my body, mind, and soul as a living sacrifice. All my issues were on the altar of the Lord.

Romans 12:1: "I beseech you therefore, brethren, by the mercies of God, that ye present your bodies a living sacrifice, holy, acceptable unto God, which is your reasonable service."

My life was a mess and a complete disaster. I put all my broken pieces on the altar and dedicated them to the Lord. I felt that I was just a piece of a human being, but I laid every broken piece on the altar. I laid all my demons on the altar! All my insanity was laid on the altar! All my anger was on the altar. I was standing there when I heard him say, "Uncover the deep things."

Psalm 42:7, "Deep calls unto deep at the noise of your waterfalls; All Your waves and billows have gone over me."

I felt the sovereign hand of the Lord God reach deep down inside my spirit and pull up something by the root. I felt physical pain as it was being removed. "Oh, oh!" I cried. I began screaming as I bent over from the agony in my soul. Oh, what a pitiful sight it was—a pitiful soul that was kicking, longing, and struggling to survive. Inside, part of me screamed, "Stop, Lord, it hurts too badly! I am afraid. Stop! I can't go through this!" The Lord God said, "Stop struggling, and let me have that issue. Let me behind that sealed door. Give it to me!" Have you ever had a tug of war with the Lord? God is so big, and we are so small, but he will only take the pain if you give it to him. Suddenly I cried out, "Yes, Lord! Take it from me, because I cannot carry this for the rest of my life. Lord, the pain is killing me. I am dying to be free! Lord, I want to live!" None could see what was happening inside me as I stood at that altar. Every ear heard me screaming and struggling in painful agony.

I received so much deliverance that Sunday, and I received enough strength to begin my healing process. The chains and shackles had to break off my feet. The demons had to get up and leave my mind, my will, and my emotions. The Lord commanded deliverance that day, and everything binding me had to leave. I did not want the demons inside me, and I was desperate to be set free.

Acts 8:7: "For unclean spirits, crying with loud voice, came out of many that were possessed with them: and many taken with palsies, and that were lame, were healed."

I had been taught from a young age that evil spirits existed. Evil spirits do not have human bodies, yet they work in our physical world. Two major spirits look at you and desire to use your body for their glory. The Lord God looks at you and desires to use your body. He desires to get inside your body, mind, soul, and spirit, and to use you for his glory. He wants to possess you to the point that you will be fully obedient and do whatever he says. God wants his kingdom to be built here on earth as it is in heaven. In God's kingdom, there is no pain, poverty, destruction, or fear. God wants to spread love, joy, peace, and happiness here on earth as it is in heaven. However, another spirit looks at you with a hateful passion and longs to use your body, mind, will, and emotions. Satan lusts for your body! He thinks of ways to get inside you and possess you. Satan desires that his kingdom come and his will be done on earth as it is in hell.

God says, "Oh, how I crave to use that body for my glory."

Satan says the same thing: "Oh, how I want to use that body to advance my evil kingdom and reign of terror."

God says, "We can save so many lives and souls with that mouth and body."

Satan says, "We could destroy so many lives with that mouth and that body. I will use her beauty to seduce men and spread AIDS and other deadly diseases. I will use her body to break many hearts after sex and perverse acts. I can use her body to act in pornographic material and lead many pitiful souls to hell."

God says, "Oh, millions of souls can be won into the kingdom with her loud voice and anointing."

All spirits need bodies to act out their desires. Did you hear what I said? All spirits need bodies to act out their passions and desires. The Bible even records that evil spirits were so desperate that they begged to go into pigs. They begged for Jesus to send them into bodies, even if they were not human. The Holy Spirit needs a human body to get his work done on earth, and so does the Devil! Which spirit are you allowing to use your body? You have to make up in your mind that you want to be set free. You have to tell the Devil that you don't want to carry him around anymore. You must refuse to be a house and a resting place for the Enemy. It does not matter how the evil spirit got inside there; you need to get him out.

John 10:10: "The thief cometh not, but for to steal, and to kill, and to destroy: I am come that they might have life, and that they might have it more abundantly."

If you have an evil spirit inside you, that spirit's one goal is to destroy you from the inside out! He wants to drive you insane and use you to destroy your own life and the lives of others. Evil spirits take advantage of your human experience. One traumatic event can be an open door for evil to enter your life. Children naturally make fun of each other. The child that is on the receiving end may develop low self-esteem. The evil spirit takes advantage of the child's low self-esteem by adding suicidal thoughts to the child's mind. Over time, the child who started out with low self-esteem ends up committing suicide because a spirit of depression took advantage of the child. In recent years, we have seen students bring guns to school and kill others before turning the guns on themselves.

If you know that you have evil spirits and deep hurt inside you, you will be more easily delivered when you open yourself up to the Lord. However, it may be painful to have to relive the past and remember where the pain started.

Sometimes we give issues up to the Lord, but we take them back as soon as we finish praying. When we let God have an issue, we need to leave it with him. That means that you stop worrying about the same issue. Don't allow the Enemy to drive you crazy! Stop listening to his voice, and command it to be silenced.

Some of you are going through mental hell and anguish. You are beating yourself up daily because of the past decisions you have made. You are violently beating yourself over and over. If you could run away from yourself, you would. You can move, but wherever you go, you are there.

> And they came over unto the other side of the sea, into the country of the Gadarenes. And when he was come out of the ship, immediately there met him out of the tombs a man with an unclean spirit, Who had his dwelling among the tombs; and no man could bind him, no, not with chains: Because that he had been often bound with fetters and chains, and the chains had been plucked asunder by him, and the fetters broken in pieces: neither could any man tame him. And always, night and day, he was in the mountains, and in the tombs, crying, and cutting himself with

stones. But when he saw Jesus afar off, he ran and worshipped him. (Mark 5: 1–6)

This man had literally been driven insane by demons. He cried out for freedom in the tombs. The Scripture shows how the man was so possessed that he was driven away from society, friends, family, work, and the life that was once normal. He sat in the tombs mutilating himself because of his pain. Just a side note: I have worked with teenagers who have cut themselves to relieve the pain they feel inside. They say things like, "I feel so much pain on the inside that cutting helps me balance it on the outside. I have to have a way to get relief!" The same spirit of mutilation that possessed this man also inhabits our teenagers who cut themselves. Cutting is a sign of great internal conflict! Also, watch out for people who feel a need to pierce almost every area of their bodies. I don't mean a few holes in the ear, but excessive piercing. This is the same spirit of mutilation that causes them to inflict pain on themselves. Some even feel the urge to burn themselves with cigarettes and other objects. There is a root and cause for the desire to cut, wound, tattoo, or inflict pain on your own body. What I rejoice over is the fact that Jesus came to where the man was and set him free from the bondage of Satan. Who else would have come to the tomb to deliver him? I am sure that many people heard him crying and yelling from the tombs, but none had the courage or power to set him free. If Jesus set this possessed man free, then I know he can deliver you! Jesus said, "Come out of him, you unclean spirit!" He is saying that same thing today! "Loosen her, and let her go!" Hey, when the Lord told that evil spirit to come out, it had to come out!

All of us have made mistakes, and we have many regrets. None of us can do anything about the past. We all wish we could go back in time and change so many pitiful decisions we have made, but we can't. What you can do is change from this day forward. Maybe you were a terrible mother, daughter, student, wife, or husband. You need to admit to yourself, God, and your family that you did not do your best. You also need to apologize and assure whomever is concerned that you can change your future decisions.

It is so important that you connect with a Spirit-filled church whose members know how to pray for your deliverance. If you don't know of any, then get out the phone book, go online, or ask the Lord to lead you to a deliverance minister. Are you ready to be set free? Has the Enemy worn you out? I was ready to kick him out of my house then, and I will be ready to chop his head off if he tries to sneak inside there again. Only the Word of God will keep him out and keep you free. Memorize the Word of God. Live the best life that you can according to the Word of God. Forgive those who have harmed you. Don't try to hide your failures and struggles from God. Those steps alone will help you make great progress in healing and restoration.

At the beginning of this chapter, I talked about drinking a whole pot of coffee. I meant that sometimes you might have to rely on God more closely than other times. I know we all need God and have to pray daily. You may have times when you don't only pray at night, but you pray several times in the same day. Most of us pray in the morning and at night. Have you ever had to pray fifteen times in a single day because you felt your mind snapping? That is what I mean by drinking a whole pot of coffee. Drink several cups of God's spirit. One cup will not do. One prayer will not do when you feel that you are losing control. One song will not do when you feel your heart breaking and feel the tears pouring from your weary eyes. Honey, you pray as many times as you need to. God does not mind hearing from you! He is faithful and just to heal you!

Matthew 7:8: "For every one that asketh receiveth; and he that seeketh findeth; and to him that knocketh it shall be opened."

I can imagine you saying, "Hey, Lord, it is me again, and again, and again." God says, "If you keep knocking, I'll keep answering! If you keep talking, I'll keep listening. If you keep crying, I'll keep wiping your tears away." God will not only see your pain, but if you ask him, he will do something about it! Drink as much coffee as you need!

I have often felt that I was like a patient whose heart had stopped beating. The sound of the heart monitor indicated that my heart was no longer beating. I was completely dead and hopeless on the inside. The spiritual doctors had done all they could do for me, and they wrote down the time of my death. The time of death was at the moment of my rape. I was dead and had no hope of revival. However, the master surgeon came in and pulled the sheet off of my body. The Creator of my soul came in and put the defibrillator on my chest anyway. He told the hopeless doctors to "crank up the electricity as high as it could go!" I lay there, surrounded by death and destruction. The master surgeon shocked me and brought me back to life. He kept shocking me until my heart started pumping as he designed it to. He shocked me until my will came in line with his will. He shocked me until death had to let me go and I began to breathe again. He shocked me until I jumped off the table and started ministering to others. He ran electricity through my entire body until I had a new attitude. Then he shined his light in my eyes to see if I had fully recovered. The master surgeon brought me back to life, and he can do the same for you. He left no sign of trauma on my life. All I have is a memory of what happened, and since he brushed my teeth, the taste of bitterness has disappeared from my mouth.

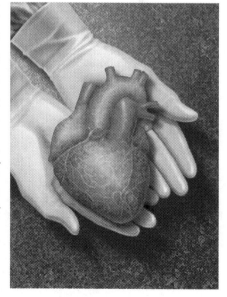

My Sister Tamar

So Amnon lay down and pretended to be ill. When the king came to see him, Amnon said to him, "I would like my sister Tamar to come and make some special bread in my sight, so I may eat from her hand."

David sent word to Tamar at the palace: "Go to the house of your brother Amnon and prepare some food for him." So Tamar went to the house of her brother Amnon, who was lying down. She took some dough, kneaded it, made the bread in his sight and baked it. Then she took the pan and served him the bread, but he refused to eat.

"Send everyone out of here," Amnon said. So everyone left him. Then Amnon said to Tamar, "Bring the food here into my bedroom so I may eat from your hand." And Tamar took the bread she had prepared and brought it to her brother Amnon in his bedroom. But when she took it to him to eat, he grabbed her and said, "Come to bed with me, my sister."

"Don't, my brother!" she said to him. "Don't force me.
Such a thing should not be done in Israel! Don't do this
wicked thing. What about me? Where could I get rid of
my disgrace? And what about you? You would be like
one of the wicked fools in Israel. Please speak to the king;
he will not keep me from being married to you." But he
refused to listen to her, and since he was stronger than
she, he raped her. (2 Samuel 13:6–14 NIV)

Why do bad things happen to good people? The fact is that God cannot be blamed when bad things happen. It hurts his heart to see how evil people carry out evil plans. People have a choice and sometimes they choose to allow Satan to use them for evil.

Genesis 6:5: "The LORD saw how great man's wickedness on the earth had become, and that every inclination of the thoughts of his heart was only evil all the time."

Oh, how I hate the fact that I can relate to Tamar's story. I recognize that millions of women and men can relate to this story. I read this story after I was a victim of an almost fatal rape. While reading my Bible, I stumbled upon this story. I said, "Oh, this is me!" I was not raped by my brother, but I felt a certain kinship to the girl in this story. We both shared feelings of injustice after being victims of rape. After the rape, I sat in a deep depression for almost two years, and I can say that those were the best and worst two years of my life. It was the worst because I was on a terrible emotional rollacoster. It was the best because I had no choice but to reach up to God for help. During that time, God was my comforter, counselor, psychiatrist and teacher. I can imagine how much pain and sorrow Tamar must have felt. Shame, sorrow, disgrace, low self-esteem, and spiritual death seem to always accompany rape and molestation. Tamar was deceived by her own brother. I know; it is bad enough if a stranger or a distant relative rapes you, but can you imagine being raped by your own brother? Incest, sex between relatives, is also widespread in the world and, sadly, in the church. This subject is painful to deal with and is rarely talked about. It is rarely dealt with properly once it is found out.

Most likely, Tamar would have come in contact with her rapist every day for the rest of her life. They knew the same people, shared the same father, and ate at the same table. She did not get to attend a court and watch the rapist get sent to jail. As a matter fact, she did not get any justice at all. The only person who came to her defense was her other brother, who killed the rapist. As a rape victim, I know the feeling of dishonor that comes with being raped. When you add injustice to your dishonor, a breakdown is soon to follow.

What actions should a parent take once she finds that her own children are having sex or that one child is molesting the other? What do you do when a rapist lives under your roof? That is a question that goes back to Adam and Eve. Cain and Able were brothers, but Cain killed his brother. It must have been terrible for Cain's parents; they were angry with him for killing his brother, but they still loved him because he was also their child. Eve nursed a future murderer. Parents, you never know what mistakes your child will make. Oh, the pain goes deep for everyone involved! Good parents should not blame themselves if they have done everything to place good moral values in their children. Children are exposed to other people, movies, and negative influences that their parents know nothing about. Don't blame yourself, but you still have to deal with the issue.

Tamar's father, King David, did not do anything. Yes, David was angry, but the Bible did not record that he took any action against his rapist son. It is not recorded that David tried to comfort his daughter. Injustice! How much pain Tamar must have experienced. The bible says that God will take care of you even if your parents leave you. (author's paraphrase).

There was no one to defend her. I have personally worked with children and adults who have been victims of violent crimes. I have noticed that victims who have at least one parent fighting for them tend to recover more quickly. I have worked with several female victims who were raped or molested by their fathers. Females recover more quickly when the female's mother takes a strong stand and prosecutes or even removes the father from the home. I have also worked with male victims of violent crimes; if a male victim's parent or parents take a strong stand to protect him, the male victim recovers more quickly than the victims who have no help from anyone. While working for Child Protective Services, I discovered that most of the children in foster care were abused sexually or physically by the very people who were supposed to care for and protect them. Someone has to fight and protect our young people. There must be some form of justice in the minds of the victims. A victim feels some comfort if someone at least tries to protect him from harm. "Mom, at least tried to defend me! Daddy at least divorced the woman who was beating me, and he took me to counseling! Grandma at least called the police when she found that someone was molesting me! My uncle at least came and picked me up when he found out Mom was on drugs! Did anyone care that I was hurting?" Do you sense a pattern in these statements above? For God's sake, *someone do something*!

I had the honor of working for Child Protective Services as a child abuse investigator. I became outraged when I had cases in which children were being abused and neglected by their Christian parents. I realized that our children are being abused in the world and in the church. There were cases in which the child would be removed from her home because of sexual abuse, be placed in a Christian foster home, and then be further abused and neglected. Parents, you must take the lead at protecting your children's hearts. Church, you can be a great, loving resource for foster children. Since they already feel unwanted, you can be a real example of Christ's love to them.

I have worked with multiple mothers who stay in abusive relationships for one reason or another. Mothers, you are putting your children in a dangerous place when you decide to continue living in an abusive relationship. You help foster bitterness and anger in your children's hearts when you allow them to see you get beaten, kicked, choked, cursed, and abused! Why are you allowing someone to abuse you and treat you as if you are not even human? When your children see you get abused, they are getting abused also. If violent acts are committed in front of your children's eyes, then they are being traumatized. We wonder why our children are not saved or interested in church. They are not saved because they saw you get beat up at home and then go to church like everything was fine. Children question the God of love. Why would he want you to stay in a marriage in which he knows you are being beaten? They wonder why God would not come to their rescue. That is not the will of God, and you are confusing the children.

Mothers, your children can legally be removed from your care if you allow yourself to stay in an abusive relationship. You can be charged for abuse if you fail to act and take them out of that traumatic situation. Fathers, if you know your wife or girlfriend is abusing your child, then you are just as guilty if you don't do anything to stop the abuse. Parents, take action and stop abusing or ignoring the abuse of your children. Often women leave their children with their own former molesters. Usually if your step-father, uncle, or brother molested you, then it would not be in your best interest to leave your children with those same people. Please find another babysitter! Christian women, are you sitting in church and leaving your daughter at home with a child molester? Is your child safe in his own bed? Mothers, can your son sleep in peace, or does he have to worry about your boyfriend sneaking in his room at night? Mom, are you so desperate for a man that you are allowing him to molest your child? I know these are hard questions, but you must answer them in court, before God, and/or in the newspaper. I am talking to all parents: *Do not allow your child to be abused so that your family will stay together! Some families don't need to stay together. If abuse, neglect, incest, and molestation are happening under your roof, your family is already split apart by lies and deceit.*

Mom, come out of denial; you usually suspect something is going on. You need to start asking questions. Stop thinking about your own security, and think about the mental stability of your child. Dad, stop thinking about getting your flesh satisfied, and deal with the issue. You know that your wife or girlfriend is verbally abusing your child. Parents, you had better put a stop to the abuse of your child, or you will be brought to open shame. God hates the abuse of children, and if you don't fight for your children, God will. Also, people who know about the abuse or suspect abuse need to intervene. If you know about it and don't do anything, you are just as guilty. There is nothing worse than the whole church knowing that a child or woman is being abused, and no one says anything! People come to church for healing. We, as the church, need to do more than pray. Sometimes we need to confront the abuser and get law enforcement involved.

Don't be like David and ignore your children's cries and pain. Take action, and do whatever it takes to get them out of a bad situation. Mothers, do you want your sons to grow up and kill your abusive husband? You could have prevented your husband's death and your son's imprisonment. Do something about it now! Father, do you want your daughter to grow up and become a teenage runaway because you allowed your wife to abuse her? Your child could wind up dead or on a milk carton because you did not stop the abuse! Parents, stop the abuse of your children. David's crime was his silence. What are you going to do, parent? Some of you owe your children an apology for not taking action sooner. I heard a women tell her children that she was sorry that she had not been a good mother. She was not "mother of the year." She apologized for exposing her children to harm and violence. She told them that now things were going to be different since she had Jesus in her heart. Her children were willing to forgive her because she admitted she had been wrong and was willing to make things right. You can do that same thing with your children, even if they are now adults. Just admit it: some of you were terrible parents and did a terrible job. If you did a bad job, just admit it. Believe me, your children will usually let you know that you were terrible. There is nothing wrong with telling your children, "I am so sorry. I was a terrible parent, and I allowed several things to happen to you that I shouldn't have. I am sorry for hurting you. I love you, and if I could go back in time to fix things, I would. I am sorry and I will never hurt you again. I knew you were hurting, and I did nothing. I hurt you.. Please forgive me for what I have done." I promise you that God will heal that relationship if you truly admit the part you played and repent from your heart. Parents, you need to repent to God and your children. Don't feel bad if they do not forgive you immediately. It could take years to rebuild that broken relationship.

David should have taken some action to protect his daughter's heart and her honor. She did not even get an apology from her brother, because he was not sorry. As a matter of fact, the Bible declares that her brother hated her after he raped her. You may not believe this, but when someone violates you, sometimes just a simple apology helps in the forgiveness process. "I am sorry for treating you badly and hurting you" goes a long way. Later on in that same chapter, Amnon told his servant to put Tamar out of his home. She was raped then pushed outside in shame.

Tamar was first degraded and then dishonored by her brother. I can hear her weeping countless days and nights. I can imagine warm, painful tears streaming down her face onto her torn plain clothes. Tamar had previously worn a dazzling, beautiful long robe of colors. Her robe symbolized that she was a proud virgin princess, Daddy's little girl, and the king's daughter. The world had not defiled her. She was a complete woman with nothing broken and nothing missing. However, after her rape, she stripped off her robe of honor and descended into a bottomless depression. The Bible is not clear as to how long she was depressed, but I know that without intervention, a victim is depressed for the rest of her life. Tamar could not say anything to anyone. She had no justice, no relief, no counseling, and no hope of healing. Tamar's other brother, Absalom, asked Tamar if she had been raped by her brother, Amnon. After she told Absalom about the terrible event, he told her to keep quiet.

That's what wrong with the church and the world today. Something terrifying and disgusting is happening under our roofs, and no one is talking about it! Victims are told to keep quiet. Some are even blamed for breaking up the family. I am here to tell you today, do not keep quiet! Do not suffer in silence, because it is not the will of God. I don't care if it happened twenty years ago. The pain is still fresh if you have not told anyone or dealt with it in private. Secrets hate to be hidden, and they have a way of oozing out one way or another. They tend to surface in your attitudes, in your dreams, in your untamed drive for success, in your bitterness, in your hatred for men, in your mistrust for women, and in your lack of love for the Lord God. It is time that we expose the Devil for who he is. He comes to steal, kill, and destroy.

When a person is raped or molested, something in him dies. It is like his joyful innocence is violently strangled to death. The good, innocent, and hopeful part of him is completely shattered, devastated, and humiliated. Open your mouth and cry out for justice! Open your mouth and cry out for mercy! Open your mouth and scream for your freedom! Open your mouth so that the Enemy of your body and soul can be punished! I know that if the law fails, the Lord God will pick up your fight. He will defend your cause. The law failed in my case because I had a worthless lawyer. I was a poor college student with no money, so the court assigned a lawyer to me. The man who raped me received ten years probation but no prison time for the crime he committed. I felt pressured to settle out of court and had no direction. Because of my emotional distress, my parents felt it would be better to settle out of court. I was in terrible condition, and my condition would have worsened if I had to see Tony again. I later regretted my decision because I felt that he walked a free man while I was locked away. If it were not for the Lord, I would have spent the rest of my life in a spiritual prison while he walked free.

Psalm 35:23: "Awake, and rise to my defense! Contend for me, my God and Lord" (NIV).

Deuteronomy 10:18: "He defends the cause of the fatherless and the widow, and loves the alien, giving him food and clothing" (NIV).

I want you to take comfort in knowing that God not only saw it, but he will do something about it. Baby, pick your head up and go on with your life. You cannot live in shame, guilt, and sorrow all your life. You can admit that it was a horrible thing that you have been through. You have every right to be angry. You have every right to feel violated and angry at the vessel that was used by the Devil. The fact is that someone was used as a vessel of Satan. Satan's goal was to destroy that good and innocent thing in you. He wanted to destroy that innocence, freedom, love, peace, and goodness inside you.

John 10:10: "The thief comes only to steal and kill and destroy; I have come that they may have life, and have it to the full" (NIV).

I was determined that I would not be like Tamar. I did not want to bury myself behind closed doors for the rest of my life. I was determined that I would not be a shattered and mangled victim forever. I would be free! I would be healed, and I would be made complete! I would be beautiful from the inside out.

> The Spirit of the Lord GOD is upon me; because the LORD hath anointed me to preach good tidings unto the meek; he hath sent me to bind up the brokenhearted, to proclaim liberty to the captives, and the opening of the prison to them that are bound; To proclaim the acceptable year of the LORD, and the day of vengeance of our God; to comfort all that mourn; To appoint unto them that mourn in Zion, to give unto them beauty for ashes, the oil of joy for mourning, the garment of praise for the spirit of heaviness; that they might be called trees

of righteousness, the planting of the LORD, that he might be glorified. (Isaiah 61:1–3)

I want you to know that even if a great injustice has been done to you, you can still live a good, peaceful, happy, fulfilled, and joyful life. With God, all things are possible. He still can get the glory out of your life. God gets glory when we come through trials and tribulations and then turn and help someone else.

Joel 2:25: "And I will restore to you the years that the locust hath eaten, the cankerworm, and the caterpiller."

If you will turn every angry, bitter feeling over to God, you have his promise that he will restore all the years you spent dealing with shame, guilt, frustration, and dishonor. God said he *will restore the years that the locust has eaten.* You may feel that no one understands what you are going through. You may have wasted years in deep anguish and mental turmoil, but God promised to restore the years that were stolen. He will restore the innocence that was stolen. He will restore the sleepless nights you have had. Your pain did not go unnoticed to God. Yes, the truth is ugly! Yes, it is painful to revisit the disgrace that you have experienced. Yes, it was wrong, and it destroyed some good things in your life, but *choose* to forgive the person who harmed you! If you do not, you are giving that person power over the rest of your life. Do you want to give Satan the satisfaction of knowing that he destroyed your life? Do you want the molester to take pride in knowing that he or she was the one who put you behind closed doors? Maybe you could not handle going to court or trial, but someone will stop the molester. It may not have been you, but it will be someone. The sad truth is that if no one stops the molester, then he or she usually continues to hurt person after person. If you get free, then God will use you to free someone else. You can still be anything God says you can be.

Isaiah 61:7: "For your shame ye shall have double; and for confusion they shall rejoice in their portion: therefore in their land they shall possess the double: everlasting joy shall be unto them."

What to Do If Incest Occurs in Your Family

Leviticus 18:9: "Do not have sexual relations with your sister, either your father's daughter or your mother's daughter, whether she was born in the same home or elsewhere" (NIV).

The entire of chapter of Leviticus 18 deals with sex between relatives. The Word of God establishes that God's law forbids it.

What to Do If Incest Occurs in Your Family

1. Acknowledge the problem and seek wise counsel.

2. The perpetrator, the one who inflicted the pain on the other, must be removed from the home. I'm not talking about permanently, but at least while the other child is healing. It could be months or even years depending on how bad the situation is.

3. It is best to find a trustworthy friend or relative with whom the child feels comfortable and whom the child trusts. If your pastor or other people that attend your church are trustworthy, they could be a safe haven for the offending child.

4. The victim and the perpetrator must both go to counseling, separately. The parents or a relative needs to go to counseling with both children.

5. The parents need to engage in much prayer and fasting. Both children and their parents need to go to their Spirit-filled leadership to seek deliverance for the family.

6. There must be boundaries set up by the parents and the victim in the home. Rules must be in place before the perpetrator can be returned to the home. Parents, don't be ignorant and think everything is okay when you feel it is not. Monitor the children's progress. If the victim is not ready to live with the perpetrator, please be sensitive. Put your child's needs before your desire to have your family back together. In this case, healing is more important than unity in the home. Be aware that your lives have been horribly interrupted and that things may be out of sorts for while.

7. You must determine who else can watch the children while you are away. The children must never be left alone from that point on. Utilize your family, friends, church members, and those who are trustworthy and familiar with the situation.

8. The counselor, the leadership, and you, parents, must determine that it is safe for the perpetrator to return to the home.

9. Now that the family has been restored, the entire family needs to be in counseling together with a counselor or spiritual leader.

God can restore any situation, but he did not say hard work would not be involved. It may take years to recover from molestation or incest in the family. However, the family must be willing to come together and agree that no matter how long it takes, they are willing to do whatever they can to make sure their child does not forever stay a victim. Parents, you can deal with it now or wait for your family to be completely destroyed in the future. It is not God's will that any should perish. Parents, it should not be your will to allow the victim or the perpetrator to perish, especially since you are responsible for your children. Slowly and prayerfully listen to what God is saying to your heart, and be open to his will for your family and for you.

Also, mothers should not stay married to a man who is having sex with his daughters or sons. Fathers should not stay married to a woman who is having sex with her sons or daughters. This includes rape, molestation, and physical abuse. The Bible forbids this, and you should too. Please don't sacrifice your child for your own selfish pleasure or financial stability. Choose your child every time! Ladies and gentlemen, do not marry a person who has ever molested or abused your children.

The Night Vision

There is no way that I could ever write this book without revealing the night vision that the Lord gave me. I was not totally asleep when suddenly I fell into a trancelike state. It was about ten months after I was raped. I was lying on my bed, and I felt the presence and power of the Lord in my room. I sensed that I was not alone in my room, and then suddenly I felt paralyzed. I heard the voice of the Lord say, "I want to show you something."

Night visions, dreams, and revealed secrets from the Lord are mentioned all through the Holy Bible. God will speak to you when you are quiet and when your mind is not constantly wandering. Sometimes, the only time we can hear from God is when we are asleep. If God cannot get a message to you, he will steal time with you. He will talk to you when your car breaks down and you are stranded on the side of the road. He will talk to you when you forgot to pay your phone bill and cannot talk to anyone. He will talk to you while lying in your hospital bed. He may break into your sleep and talk to you at a time when you should be at peace.

Job 4:12–17: "Now a thing was secretly brought to me, and mine ear received a little thereof. In thoughts from the visions of the night, when deep sleep falleth on men, Fear came upon me, and trembling, which made all my bones to shake. Then a spirit passed before my face; the hair of my flesh stood up: It stood still, but I could not discern the form thereof: an image was before mine eyes, there was silence, and I heard a voice, saying, Shall mortal man be more just than God? shall a man be more pure than his maker."

In this vision, I saw a little girl standing alone in what appeared to be a secret room. The child was about six years old, and I wondered why the child had no adult supervision. I saw a man appear in front of the child. He was wearing a long black cape. The cape covered the man's head all the way down to his feet. I looked very closely as the man slowly removed his entire cape in front of the child. To my astonishment, what I saw was not a man at all; it was a hideous creature. The creature had the body of a skeleton, face of a man, long blond hair, large female breasts, and a huge male penis. It appeared to exhibit a mixture of male and female characteristics. I watched in horror as this creature began to molest and then rape the child in front of my eyes. The creature was on top of the female child when he began to penetrate her small female vagina. I don't know how else to relate what I saw except to tell you exactly how it was shown to me. This may be graphic, but what is happening to our children is graphic. What happened in your family was graphic, and what we see on television is graphic. Life is filled with graphic material, and life is raw and uncut. There is power in small details. I need to let you know what I saw for you to understand.

Out of the creature's penis shot what appeared to be large amounts of pure black ink directly into the female's vagina. The next thing I saw made me weak at my knees. I watched as the black ink turned into small lively spiders. I watched as the spiders traveled up into the female's uterus, ovaries, and stomach. The spiders seemed to grab a tight hold on these areas of the female's body. The creature left the child after it had finished raping her. I didn't know what to do for the child, because I was still gazing at what had just happened. To my surprise, the child began to grow into a beautiful woman in front of my eyes. She grew slowly, but to my shock, as she grew, so did the spiders inside her. I watched as one spider grew so large that it took over the now adult female's body. I heard a voice say, "The spirit can fully use her now that she is old enough to be used."

My eyes opened, and I became aware that I was back in my bedroom. I was very troubled and prayed for the meaning of the vision. What the Lord revealed to me was astounding as so true.

The Lord showed me a husband and wife loving and holding each other. I saw that when the man releases his seed into his wife, the seed is white. If you have taken any type of biology class, you will remember that male sperm is white as soon as oxygen hits it. The semen is red (blood) inside the male's body but turns white once it hits the air. That white semen is what produces life inside the female. The male sperm connects with the female egg, and boom! Nine months later we have a beautiful baby. Remember that in my vision I told you that something like black ink shot out of the creature's penis? That creature shot spirits of death into the female child's reproductive organs! The small spiders were spirits that attached themselves to the very places that she would need to bring life into the world. The spirits came inside her through molestation and rape. The Lord revealed to me that the creature was a spirit of lust and perversion. It had mixed characteristics because this evil, demonic spirit attacks males and females alike. It has no restrictions or boundaries as to whom it violently attacks. There is a spirit of lust and perversion running rampant in our homes, churches, families, and with our children. When this spirit is injected into a child, it cannot fully use the child's body at that time. But, you see, as the child grows physically, so does the spirit's influence over the child. A six-year-old child can not bear children, prostitute, or willingly participate in pornography videos, but an eighteen-year-old can do all of those things. The spirit waits until it can unleash its desires and hurt on others. Therefore, the adult victim will either molest and rape others or will become so angry that she will hurt others. These days, the demons are too desperate to wait. Children as young as eight years old are molesting others, and some are killing other children.

Lying there, I saw a door opened into my own heart. I watched my own molestation at the age of seven years old. I was taken back to the evening that my parents dropped my siblings and me off at their fellow church members' home. Our families were very close, and their children were close to our family. We all went into the oldest son's room to watch television. I lay at the head of the bed with the sixteen-year-old young man because my other siblings were sitting on the foot of the bed, watching television. The young man put the cover over us, and when no one was watching, he put his hand up my private area. I remember feeling such great pain, but I did not know what was happening. I felt something break inside me. Later I realized that young man had taken my virginity. I was so young and did not know about "good touches and bad touches." I did not tell anyone what happened. That same young man had been molested himself by older adults.

I watched as another door was opened in my heart. That night, about a year later, a church member's granddaughter spent the night with my sisters and me. The girl was about fourteen years old at the time, and I was eight years old. When everyone was outside, she took me into my room and violently molested me. I cannot even discuss in this book what she did to me. I remembered feeling such physical pain. I did not know what to do, and I did not tell anyone. That same young lady was molested as a child and was being abused by her older brother.

Another time, children from our church came over and molested me in our bathroom. Do you see a pattern there? I was consumed with lust after those experiences, and I began to crave sexual contact. You know there is no logical explanation for an eight-year-old child to crave sex, unless she has been exposed to it. Children mimic some things they see on television, but if the child is going into graphic sexual detail, you'd better be worried! My parents had no idea these things happened to me because I did not tell them. I did not tell them of the passion and desires that I had burning within me. A demon had entered into me as a child because of molestation. The lust that burned inside me was a spirit. The Lord revealed to me that that spirit had been hiding in there all the time. It was just waiting for a chance to use my body, to act out its will. God intervened, and I was delivered from that demon. Thank God for freedom.

Parents pride themselves in knowing that their children will tell them when they are hurt. No matter how much you have taught your children to tell you if someone is touching them, sometimes they will not tell for one reason or another. Parent, you are not God, and you may not know who or what has touched your child. When you ask him, you'd better be prepared for the answer.

The Lord unlocked the door of my memory because I needed to remember in order to deal with those locked away issues. Remember when I mentioned that the Lord said to open the door so that he could get deep inside? He not only opened the present, but he opened the painful locked-away memories. I knew this was the Lord showing me what happened to me as a child. I had spent most of my high school years proud to be a virgin and often prided myself in being undefiled, unlike the other girls. I did remember that immediately after I was raped, I was in pain, but I noticed there was not much blood. I realized at that very moment that I was not a virgin. I think that hurt me almost as much as being a victim of rape. I was so confused; if the man who raped me did not take my virginity, then who did? Only God could show me who took it and when.

People, you may have to go back in order to go forward. There is no use in thinking that you can just get over it. Get over what? Sometimes you don't know what happened yourself. Pray and ask the Lord to reveal any secret or painful roadblocks in your life. Let God heal them so that you can move forward in your recovery. I needed to be delivered from years of pain and anguish.

So many things can happen to those who have been victims of violent crimes. Some females who have been victims of abuse have trouble getting pregnant or have a lot of unwed, unplanned pregnancies. They often have severe menstrual cramps, some turn to lesbianism because they were hurt by males, and some are so bitter that they hate men or don't trust anyone. That is the reason that the spiders clutched onto the female reproductive organs; that is the area of healthy reproduction. When men are molested or raped, some of them turn to homosexuality, become rapists themselves, become drug addicts to numb the pain, try to become super successful, or become bitter and do not trust anyone. I was surprised to discover that many trauma survivors had parents who were also victimized. The cycles of pain seemed to pass on from one person to another. The Bible calls these cycles *curses*.

A generational curse can be passed down from one generation to another. Parents can curse their own child by saying the child is stupid, worthless, and unwanted. "I hate you. I wish you were born dead. I don't want you. You are ugly just like your father. You are a little whore just like your mother. I wish you were never born. I wish I could choke you until you die." Imagine a strong adult holding a fragile, lively newborn pup. The hands slowly yet violently choke the playful, soft puppy. Imagine a strong adult ignoring the weak whimper for help. Picture the strong person squeezing tighter and tighter until the tiny pup ceases to breathe. I know that is hard to imagine, but that is what harsh words will do to a young, innocent child. Words can heal, or they can completely destroy the innocence and very soul of a child or adult.

Leviticus 26:39: "Those of you who are left will waste away in the lands of their enemies because of their sins; also because of their fathers' sins they will waste away" (NIV).

A curse can be passed down by a parent's words, actions, or abuse. We need healthy, happy, and lively children and not mangled, abused, and demented children. Most serial killers were abused as children or had terrible upbringings. Miserable adults construct miserable children. Battered adults usually produce battered, abused children. Alcoholic adults usually produce alcoholic adult children. Someone has to step up, change her ways, and ask Jesus to break the curse over her family. It can be stopped before anyone else gets hurt, but only the blood of Jesus can stop it.

Jeremiah 31:28–29: "'Just as I watched over them to uproot and tear down, and to overthrow, destroy and bring disaster, so I will watch over them to build and to plant,' declares the LORD. 'In those days people will no longer say, "The fathers have eaten sour grapes, and the children's teeth are set on edge." Instead, everyone will die for his own sin; whoever eats sour grapes—his own teeth will be set on edge'" (NIV).

The evil spirits and actions of one generation are transferred from one person to another. How do people get sexually transmitted diseases? Millions of babies are born every day with drugs in their systems. Why? The pregnant mother used drugs, so the baby is born addicted to drugs. The child suffered from what his mother did. One person with a disease has sex with someone else. The person with the disease transfers it to the other person. If this can happen in the natural, then it can happen in the spirit! Children who are molested often become molesters. One person transfers the evil, wicked, hurtful spirit inside of her to the other person.

The same transference of spirits can happen in a way good constructive way. Blessed parents can transfer blessing to their child. An anointed spirit-filled pastor can transfer that anointing to his members. A generational blessing can be passed down from one generation to the other.

Genesis 27:7: "Bring me some game and prepare me some tasty food to eat, so that I may give you my blessing in the presence of the LORD before I die" (NIV).

Deuteronomy 34:9: "Now Joshua son of Nun was filled with the spirit of wisdom because Moses had laid his hands on him. So the Israelites listened to him and did what the LORD had commanded Moses" (NIV).

We have to speak the blessing of the Lord God over our children no matter how old they are. We must break the generational curses over our children and ourselves. Only the authority of Jesus Christ can destroy the curse. Jesus took every curse upon himself on the cross of Calvary. In the Old Testament, if the head of the family did something against the law of God, then his whole family would pay for the sin. Thanks to Jesus' sacrifice, people will die for their own sins, and everyone will give account for his own soul. You don't have to be an alcoholic because your parent was an alcoholic. We all know that if your parent was a drug abuser, you are more likely to be an abuser. Don't even open the door. All the curse needs is an open door to continue its evil reign. Ladies, if your husband has been in and out of jail, you need to intervene the first time your son starts to get in trouble with the law. Don't just say, "We are going down this road again." Stop it in its tracks! You don't have to be mentally unstable because your parent was mentally unstable. I have worked as a caseworker for those with mental health disorders. I was surprised that most people with mental illness pass their mental illness down to their children. Some of it is genetic, but some people had such trauma in childhood that they developed mental illness. Severe continued traumatic experiences can cause mental illness in your child. That does not have to happen. You don't have to sexually molest because you were molested nor do you have to live with your molestation's effects for the rest of your life.

Without accepting the Lord Jesus Christ as your Lord and Savior, you will be under the curse of your family forever. The curse will travel through every generation until every life is destroyed and everyone is dead. Don't let the curse annihilate you or your family. Stand up and tell every family curse that it stops now! Every Christian has the power and authority to tell the curse to end in the name of Jesus Christ.

My mother was a victim of several molestations in her young life. I also found out that several of my female and male relatives were victims of rape or molestation. When my parents picked me up from college after the rape, my mother was completely devastated. During my first season of healing, it was my father who stayed up with me at night and comforted me, not my mother. My mother would attempt to comfort me, but she seemed almost as devastated as I was. She cried and cried as she looked at the pain I was in. I almost wanted to comfort her during my season of healing. She later told me that she had been raped several times and was even forced to marry the man that raped her when she was an adult. You see, my father was my mother's second husband. Years earlier, she used to attend a church in Kansas. She was a single young woman at a growing, thriving church in the early 1970s. A young handsome man met my mother and wanted to take her out on a date. She was not interested in him because she was content being single and loving the Lord. One day, the young man came to her home, seeming friendly and harmless. She let him inside, since he was also a believer in Christ and a church member. She told me that suddenly the man's face took on the appearance of an animal, and he began violently raping her. The rape lasted for about two hours, and she was hurt and devastated! She was ashamed, but she did call the police. She also called her pastor's wife. The pastor's wife insisted that it was her fault for inviting him in; she would be put out of the church or she must marry this young man. She told them that he violently raped her, but that did not seem to matter. She later realized that she should have left that church. That was not of God, but she didn't know that at the time. In confusion, my mother agreed to marry the young man, who she hated and utterly despised.

During their marriage, the young man raped and physically abused my mother. She hated him and would often think of ways to kill him. Bitterness took control of her life, and she was miserable. She said that the night after she married him, she heard a voice say, "Have it annulled! Have it annulled!" She did not because she didn't know that it was God talking to her. God had not joined them, and there was nothing holy about that matrimony. She finally decided to divorce the young man. However, my mother found out that she was pregnant with the young man's child! The court said she could not divorce him until after the baby was born. The only thing good that came out of that relationship was a beautiful baby girl. The child brought much healing and joy to my mother. Thank God that something beautiful came out of that mess.

After my mother told me her story, I realized that a curse had been passed down to me. By looking at my situation, she seemed to be looking at herself being raped again. One day, she had watched me suffer long enough. She was suffering watching me suffer. My mother laid hands on me and said, "All right, Devil, this curse stops here! You have raped me, my daughters, my relatives, and you molested my son! I am sick of you terrorizing my family. This curse stops here and now. I decree in the name of Jesus that the curse of rape and molestation is broken off my family and future generations. The curse will not continue. Jesus took all the curses of the world on his shoulders, and by his blood I have been set free. I break this curse off my family in Jesus' name! I call for the blessings of God over this child and all my family in Jesus' name. Lord, let every blessing choke out and destroy every curse. I curse the unholy seeds of everything that has been planted in my family. The unholy seeds will not grow up and develop any further. I call for the fruit of the Holy Spirit to come forth in Jesus' name."

I prayed the prayer and broke the curse off all the children and relatives that I will have in the future. No matter what the curse is in your family, you can pray a similar prayer. The curse does not have to continue. Look for patterns in your family history, as that is usually where the curse is. Is alcoholism ruining your family? Are the men in and out of jail? Does cancer run from person to person? Is there a pattern of failure in your family or a pattern of people who just can't seem to get themselves together? If you don't stop it in Jesus' name, then the curse will continue until you and your family are completely destroyed. Break it before it breaks you. Destroy it, before it can destroy you. Rebuild your home and family brick by brick.

Luke 10:19: "Behold, I give unto you power to tread on serpents and scorpions, and over all the power of the enemy: and nothing shall by any means hurt you."

Steps to Spiritual Healing

Let's focus on the process of spiritual healing. Imagine that you go to an extremely tall building. Most of us would not climb twelve staircases by choice, we would try to find the nearest elevator. What would you do if the elevator was broken? Most likely you would take the stairs. If you are like me, you probably do not like climbing long staircases to get to where you need to go. There are times when the elevator may be broken in a large building. You know you have to get to the twelfth floor, so you ask, "Where are the stairs?" You stand at the bottom of the staircase and examine how many stairs you will have to climb to get to the twelfth floor. Whatever you need is on the twelfth floor. You make a choice to turn back and wait until they fix the elevator or to start climbing so that you will reach your destination.

Years ago, my sisters and I went to visit my grandfather in Kansas. I'd always loved my grandfather's long staircase. He had a two-story home, and his long carpeted stairs were my favorite part of his house. My nine-month-old nephew, Samuel, was beginning to make attempts to walk at that time. One day I was downstairs watching Samuel. My sister was upstairs, preparing to go to the mall. We talked back and forth, even though I was downstairs and she was upstairs. My nephew could hear his mother's voice, but he did not know where she was located. He began to follow the sound of her voice as he inched closer and closer to her sound. Finally, I watched him crawl and sit at the bottom of the staircase. He realized that she was upstairs, but he could not figure out how he would get to her. He sat there, seeming to ponder how he would get up the stairs and to his mother. What a dilemma for someone with such short legs. I waited to see what he would do. Samuel sat there, examining the stairs very carefully. He began to pull himself up the stairs by placing one knee on the lower stair and his little hand on the upper stair. He slowly crawled up one stair at a time. Of course, I was there in case he tumbled downward. My nephew reached halfway and then stopped due to pure exhaustion. His short legs could take him no further. He began to look to the top of the stairs and cry loudly for his mother. Samuel could not talk, but he seemed to say, "Mommy, I am trying to get to where you are. I can't make it by myself. Please come and pick me up!" My sister instantly responded to the cry of her son. She rushed down and said, "How did you get up here?" She met him halfway and she picked him up and carried him the rest of the way. Finally, he was in the same room with his mother.

When you are going through any kind of recovery, in a way you are at the bottom of the stairs. You have a goal at the top,

which is to recover whatever you lost. You may have lost loved ones, finances, sanity, spirituality, and possibly years of your life. Whatever you need is at the top of the stairs. First you must realize that the elevator to recovery is permanently broken. There are no quick, short, or easy ways to reach your goal of healing. You stand there, examining the long staircase. You count the stairs and wonder if the climb is going to be worth it. Of course it is worth it! Either you start climbing the stairs to healing, or you can remain miserable, heartbroken, bitter, and lonely for the rest of your life. If I were you, I would start climbing. The good thing is that the Lord God is climbing with you, and he is at the top of the stairs. If you fall and feel that you cannot make it any further in your journey of healing, he will respond to your cries. He will carry you the rest of the way. How do you recover? You will recover one step at a time.

God will respond when you first set your mind to change. He will respond when you desire to make changes in your life. He has already sent help to guide you on this journey of recovery. You will have a turning point on your road to recovery. I promise that you will feel yourself getting better.

During my season of pain, I often lay in bed unable to sleep. About one year after my rape, I had made some progress on the road to recovery. I lay there watching the Trinity Broadcasting Network (TBN). I would usually wake up around the same time in the early morning. I was still having nightmares, but they were less violent than before. About three in the morning, I lay there with tears in my eyes. I awoke from another painful nightmare, and the sweat dripped from my forehead. Jan Crouch, the cofounder of TBN, was giving her testimony. She was telling how she had been in a season of depression years earlier. She cried bitterly as she told her story of not being able to bring herself out of depression. Here she was, a powerful, smart woman of God, who fell into depression. She hid inside her home and could not bring herself to help her husband run the television station. She lay inside her own home with her hair uncombed, makeup off, and tears in her eyes. I could so relate to her pain, because I was at that same place in my life. I lay there crying, depressed, ashamed, and hidden in my home. I was just like Jan! As she told her story, she began to smile. She laughed as she told how she lost focus on her own pain. She went to church one day and saw a young lady crying bitterly at the altar. The young lady was obviously in agony of the soul, and she was alone. Jan wondered how she could help her when she was so deep in depression herself. She took steps toward the young lady and then began to pray for her. God healed her when she reached out to someone else. I began to cry, realizing that I was drowning in my own pain. I can never tell her how much that testimony helped me. After watching her testimony, I slowly began to breathe. I took a deep breath and realized that one band of bondage had fallen off. I fell asleep feeling that I was going to make it out of my pain.

The next night I awoke from another terrible nightmare. I lay there unable to sleep with sweat dripping off my forehead. I prayed that God would soon deliver me. Another life-changing program came on TBN. Bishop T. D. Jakes was preaching a sermon called, "It's Not My Will to Be Like This." He was preaching from John chapter 5, the story of the man who lay at the pool of Bethesda. An angel of the Lord would come down and stir up the water once a season. All who stepped in were healed. Most Christians have read about the man who lay at the pool of Bethesda for thirty-eight years. Jesus asked the man if he wanted to get well. At first the man said that he had no one to help him get into the pool, but he then told Jesus that he did want to get well. Jesus told the man to take up his bed and walk, and he did. The man became well because he wanted to get well, and Jesus wanted that for him too.

I cannot preach or even write all that Bishop T. D. Jakes said, but the words provided a great deliverance for me. He told about one of his old church members who had a devastating stroke. He went to the hospital to pray and encourage the woman, but when he entered her room, she was encouraging herself. The woman was trying to lift her arm and tell her damaged arm that it would work in Jesus' name. She kept speaking life to herself even though her situation seemed hopeless. The woman had a will to live, survive, be healed, and move freely. The woman became well, and she had a full recovery. It was not her will to draw up and die; she had the desire to recover, and she did. I lay there crying yet hearing the shackles fall off my own feet. I said out loud, "I want to be free; I have a will to be free. It is not my will to be depressed and hide in my own pain." I decided that after hearing the message, I would not hide any longer. I heard a message that made my soul respond, and to my surprise, I felt myself struggling to rise up.

Whenever I tell people my story, people often ask what the turning point was on my road to recovery. My season of hopelessness finally came to an end when I began to extend help to one young lady in my church. I had watched her change drastically for some time, but I could not seem to reach out to help her. One Sunday, I focused on her face and noticed a similar expression between us. She displayed sudden unhappiness, sudden weight gain, frozen emotions, and sudden withdrawal. We shared a painful silence; however, I was twenty-two and she was only ten years old. That Sunday, it seemed as if someone had sat a mirror directly in front of my eyes. For one moment, I took my attention off my own misfortune and inside agony. I did not like what was happening to her or to me. One day, I decided to talk with her relatives, and they confirmed my worst fear. They suspected that her father was molesting her. I found the time to talk to the child in private and suspicions were confirmed. Through a process, her parents divorced, and her father was removed from the home. The girl's mother did not catch the warning signs that her daughter gave. She was a good mother, but she just did not notice the changes in her child.

Parents, please pay attention to your children. They often give you hints that something is happening in their lives. Watch for small changes in them, such as loss of appetite, sudden weight gain, extreme fear, isolation, sadness, bed-wetting, and poor judgment. Christians, please don't be so spiritual that you don't notice the physical changes in your children. If your child had been friendly with someone and suddenly he or she has a dislike for that person, then something is wrong. If your child is suddenly afraid to go to daycare or school, something is wrong. If an adult wants to spend time alone with just one child all the time, something is wrong. Pay attention to your children, and notice signs they give you. Children cannot always say, "Mom, someone is hurting me. Someone told me that if I told, he was going to kill my family." Children do not have the vocabulary or knowledge to fully express what they are going through. You are the parent, guardian, relative, or caring adult. As adults, it is our job to notice and track how our children are growing and developing. Help them, because they cannot help themselves.

Helping the young girl in my church began to breathe new life into my soul. I began to live, but only on life support. Like fresh water for a dehydrated, dying man, that child pumped new life into my shattered soul. Many girls began to approach me to ask for help and freedom from their own pain. Many had heard about my rape and wanted help out of their own personal pain. By the end of that year, I slowly began to help young ladies keep themselves safe. How could I help anyone? What support could I offer anyone? Could my history serve as a present for them? Could anyone benefit from my experiences? It was final; there was no choice but to help. My friends Rosa and Evon and I began a girls' support group, DIVAS (Divinely Inspired Vessels with Anew Spirit). We talked about everything from rape to hairstyles. All the girls in our group had been raped or molested at least once in their lives. They were all under sixteen years old. Unknown to the girls, they began to be my life support machines, and they breathed into me.

During the third year, I started to take breaths on my own. I lived and began to breathe without pain. I knew that I was healed once I began to sing. Before I left for senior college, I had been the song leader at my church. I loved to write songs and praise God because he is good and his mercy endures forever. The Enemy had silenced my voice after the rape, and I could no longer sing. One day as I drove, I heard words in my mind that I had never heard before. I started singing the song that God gave me. "Lord let your glory fill this temple. You reign, you super reign, Lord, you reign. Down comes revelation; now we understand. Built on the true foundation, Lord, it's in your mighty plan. Lord, we are so simple; glory fill this temple; Lord, let your glory fall. When his glory falls, we have victory. His glory falls. Lord, you set your children free. Lord we are so simple; glory fill this temple; Lord, let your glory fall." I sang loud, and I sang free. I had more passion once I started singing again. I had passion because the Lord is good, and his mercy endureth forever.

Pride, honor, and strength had been restored inside my soul. The Christian Bible says in Psalm 23 that God would restore one's soul. How could God restore your soul if it was never broken? How can he set you free if you have never been a captive? I gained experience, love, and a new outlook on life. Actually, my soul was severely damaged the night that I became a victim of rape. Not only did my Creator restore my soul, but he also added experience for the sake of others. My girls have all grown up, and some have made their own mistakes in life. I am still around them, and they call me when needed. One thing they know is that God can and will restore you once you have been harmed.

Many people carry around pain from old traumatic events You must decide whether you are ready to start recovering or not. We already know that acting like there is not a problem, is a problem. Forgetting about what happened instead of focusing on the issue is a terrible idea. Your heart still remembers that it was hurt. Your heart, emotions, and mind cannot heal on their own. You need help to heal. You need help to survive and live a great, victorious life. Since there is no quick way to recover, you might as well decide that you are in this for the long haul. You have so many good years left, and it is time you start enjoying them. How do you recover? You take one step at a time. You must examine the stairs and decide that the climb is going to be worth it. You bet it is! If you do not have Jesus Christ as the head of your life, however, then you have no hope of real recovery. It is not going to be easy. There is no subject too nasty, painful, or disgusting to talk about. My question is, "Did it happen?" If it happened, then you need to talk about it and resolve it. Ask him to come into your heart and live inside you. Remember, he already knows what happened, and he is with you every step of the way. If you don't know how to pray, I will help you. Pray the following:

> Lord God, in the name of your son Jesus, I don't understand why bad things have happened to me. I am still so angry about so many things that have happened in my life. Lord God, please come into my heart and save my soul. I realize that I am a sinner in need of a Savior. I understand that you have all the keys to my happiness and healing. Help me forgive all of those who have hurt me. Please forgive me for all the people whom I have hurt also. Lead me through this time of recovery, and show me the things that I need to remember and deal with. Okay, Lord, I am ready to deal with my issues, and I understand that they cannot be ignored any longer. Thank you, Lord. I believe that you are the Son of God, were born of a virgin, died for my sins, and rose again so that I could have eternal life. You are alive and well in me. Amen.

Romans 10:9: "That if you confess with your mouth, 'Jesus is Lord,' and believe in your heart that God raised him from the dead, you will be saved" (NIV).

I thank God for setting me free from lust, pain, shame, guilt, and so many other bondages. I realize that if I had not been a victim of rape, I could never have developed the passion to help others who have been through it. God is so awesome because he will use your pain to help others. Did God want me to go through that terrible experience? No, he didn't. God is good, and he takes the bad things and makes them work for us. You can't lose with Jesus on your side! I have a greater love and sensitivity to others who have been victims of violent crimes. I have a greater commitment to free those who are bound by Satan. It is time that the body of Christ get healed and set free.

After I graduated from college, I became a mental health caseworker. I worked with children and adults who suffered with depression and other mental health issues. I realized that traumatic events in childhood could cause mental problems once the child became an adult. Later, I was employed as a child abuse investigator. I saw case after case of children being abused, neglected, and sexually molested. In some cases, several people knew that the child was being abused, but no one said anything. The law could not intervene and rescue the child because all the adults denied that anything was wrong. In some cases, the mother would go back to her child's abuser and molester after the case was closed. The father would go back to the woman who beat his sons and daughters. Come on, people, God is not pleased with those things, and the cycle goes on and on. God is the judge of all, and he sees everything. I am a witness that you can recover from any damage that the Enemy has done. God repairs, binds, heals, and comforts us all. It is time for you to get healed and start moving on. Forgive whom you need to, repent to those you have hurt, get the counseling you need, and let's get healed! Are you ready to start the healing process? *Okay, on your mark ... get ready ... get set ... go!*

First of all, you may need professional counseling to help you get started. You may not always be able to find a Christian counselor, but try. If you cannot find a Christian counselor, then find one who is sensitive and helpful (most are). You can start with your pastor, trustworthy friends, or a counselor in the community where you live. If you do not have insurance or can't afford to pay for counseling, your pastor would be a great person to start with. You can also check your phone book to see if there are any counselors who will give you a discount. Also, the Bible does not say it is a sin or disgrace to take medication when needed. Don't forget that Luke, one of Jesus' followers was believed to be a doctor. In some cases, people in your family might say, "You'll get over it. You don't need to take any medication or talk to anyone. Just get over it like I did!" That is not correct. The truth is, some people seem to get through pain easier than others, and some just suffer in silence. You may need more help than someone else. That does not make you weaker; it makes you different. We will all be better off once we stop comparing ourselves to others. You may need medication at least for a while if you are having difficulty sleeping, can't focus, can't get out of bed, are hopeless, are helpless, are overwhelmed with guilt, or if you basically cannot function. Please keep in mind that medication does not change what happened, but it can help you feel strong enough to deal with the situation. Taking medication and talking to someone does not make you weak. It does not make you less spiritual. It does not mean that you are any less of a Christian. It makes you smart enough to realize that you need help. Most people take medication for physical problems. Well, emotions are mental, but some medication can help you feel better. If help is available, take it!

Looking back on my painful recovery experience, I know that I could have benefited from some kind of medication or at least more intensive counseling. I did not know how to help myself. My family did what they could, but they did not know about crisis centers, rape hotlines, mental health clinics, or things of that nature. Most people do not know about the resources in their areas. All we had was Jesus, and he came through for me! By the grace of God, I made it! I've often felt as if I were a soldier who was wounded on the battlefield of life. I would have died from my injuries if I had not made it to the hospital in time. No one knew how to truly get me the help that I needed to survive. My only choice was to limp my way to the Great Physician. I bled all the way, but I made it, and you can too. Don't just think you will get healed one way. Some people need God, the doctor, and the counselor, and there is nothing wrong with that. Just get help! You may have to follow these steps several times.

1. Pray every day, and make a decision to turn the pain over to God.

2. You were a victim and played no part in it, forgive yourself for "feeling guilty" for something that you had no control over.

3. Write down everything that you can remember about the painful event.

4. Write down how the event still makes you feel. For example, "I feel so angry," and/or "I feel so bitter …"

5. Review the event, and say goodbye to the pain associated with it.

6. It may sound strange, but you can even have a small funeral for the event: "This horrible event happened to me. I did not mean for this to happen. I can't believe that it happened, but I accept that it did happen. Today I will lay this pain to rest for good. It will never come back to haunt me anymore. Everything dead needs to be buried. I take back control and will not be a victim to pain and grief anymore. I will move on with my life."

7. Get involved with a good spirit-filled church (if you are not already) that teaches about deliverance and real life issues.

8. Get outside and go for walks, swims, and relaxing drives, and go to museums, listen to good music, and go to places that show you God's beauty and glory. What good thing did you enjoy doing before you became severely depressed? Painting? Running?

9. Write down all the things that you have going right in your life.

10. Make a list of things that you hope to accomplish in this life. You will see that your list is filled with desires that you can accomplish. (go back to college, get new job, build a better relationship with my children, etc).

11. Find someone else to reach out to and help. You can work in your church, a local homeless shelter, the local Salvation Army, a hospital, etc.

12. Keep a diary of your recovery, and talk to yourself as well: "I will not be depressed. The lord will lighten my darkness. The Joy of the Lord is my strength!"

13. Read your Bible every day. There are great Psalms for dealing with depression. The entire book of John is great to read, too—especially chapters 14 and 15.

14. Eat healthy, balanced meals, and get eight hours of sleep a night. Do not get in the trap of sleeping all day because you lack motivation. Get up!

15. Resist isolation, and try to be around other people as much as possible. If you live alone, go to Wal-Mart or

the grocery store (every day if needed) just to be around other people. Go to a good church to get strength from other positive believers. God will heal you, and you can have a great life after any trauma. He did it for me, and I know he can do for you!

Useful Verses

2 Samuel 22:3 (AMP)

My God, my Rock, in Him will I take refuge; my Shield and the Horn of my salvation; my Stronghold and my Refuge, my Savior— You save me from violence.

Isaiah 60:18 (AMP)

Violence shall no more be heard in your land, nor devastation or destruction within your borders, but you shall call your walls Salvation and your gates Praise.

Jeremiah 22:3 (AMP)

Thus says the Lord: Execute justice and righteousness, and deliver out of the hand of the oppressor him who has been robbed. And do no wrong; do no violence to the stranger or temporary resident, the fatherless, or the widow, nor shed innocent blood in this place.

2 Samuel 22:49 (AMP)

Who brought me out from my enemies. You also lifted me up above those who rose up against me; You delivered me from the violent man.

2 Samuel 22:29 (AMP)

For You, O Lord, are my Lamp; the Lord lightens my darkness.

Psalm 71:21 (AMP)

Increase my greatness (my honor) and turn and comfort me.

Poems

When God Drinks Coffee with Me

He found me all broken,
I was shattered in pieces,
But he restored my beauty,
And he put me back together.
Now every time I talk with him,
Every night that I dream of him,
Every word that I get from him
Is precious.
Then words are released, and songs are given.
Promises are made when God drinks coffee with me.
I remind him of his promises;
He reminds me of his faithfulness.
I remind him that I treasure him;
He reminds me that he loves me.
I answered his invitation;
Then he answered my invitation.
Our quiet time is precious
To both of us.
Now every time I talk with him,
Every night that I dream of him,
Every word that I get from him,
Is precious. Then words are released, and songs are given;
Promises are made, when God drinks coffee with me.

My Country

In my country, we live east of the sun. We see friends and enemies
at the local Wal-Mart. We hire the disabled because they make good
greeters at the front Door. Can work, say Hello? We'll hire!
We live east of the sun.
Only here, in my country,
Do they take food stamps at the local gas station.
Did I see hot pickles, hog-head cheese, hot links, pig feet, bar-be-cue,
and fried pies at the checkout counter?
In my country, we love the drive-thru window.
May I have a chicken breast and corn, please?
Sorry, we're out! Wings and okra, please?
Sorry we're out! What do you have?
A drumstick and beans! I'll take it!
Sorry, we're closed! In my country, a condiment is a dirty word.
We still respect old hometown heroes,
We still call a judge, *Judge*, long after his retirement,
We love our Dallas Cowboys in all seasons.
In my country,
The good ole boys still meet on Saturday night at Applebee's.
Having a baby is always a personal accomplishment;
Weddings and funerals are the talk of the town.
We still go to church on Sundays.
We love God and family above our careers.
We live east of the sun,
In my country, we smile at strangers but wonder who they are.
We strive for college but support the guys who tried and failed.
Legal work is good work.
Good ole East Texas.
My country is east of the sun.

The Keeper of the Garden

Ruined, ruined; I knew my garden was completely demolished!

I had worked so hard planting seeds, watering seeds, pruning bushes, and pulling out weeds in my sacred garden. This was my special place that I took pride in. I had raised the most beautiful flowers that eyes could see. I cherished the prize-winning orchids, daisies, roses that man could name. This garden was the paradise of God, and it was the place where he came to lay his head. My garden was indeed extraordinary. I stared at it daily, basking in the beauty and glory, and I became the keeper of the garden. I did not have the mark of Cain, because the ground was easy to till. The soil was rich, fertile, and gave much more than I could ever ask. As the keeper of the garden, I felt it my duty to protect it from the harm of strangers. I guarded it as if it were an infant in need of protection. One day, to my surprise, someone had forced his way into my garden. In anguish and despair, I fell to my knees. In a heap of tears, I questioned why. Crawling into the remains of what once was mine. I knew that my beautiful flowers could never be replaced. Huge footprints, signs of jerking tender flowers, dirty handprints, and signs of lifeless beauty were all that remained. "Oh, God, someone has destroyed my perfect garden. I have failed to protect the beautiful flowers that you gave me," I said. Sobbing to the core of my soul, my body trembled. No words could describe the grief and agony of my heart. Several sensations rushed through my body. Disbelief, anger, vexation, helplessness, and hatred all appeared to be fighting for the top position. "My garden can never be replaced; it is ruined forever. I don't have the strength or the seeds to plant another perfect garden." Then in the warm, soothing voice of the only the captain of my soul came the response. It came in the warm breeze that was sent to dry my tears. It came in the broken petals as they caught the sweat that ran down my face. It came in the soil that healed the wounds on my knees. Then his voice came out as the whistle of the wind. "Child, your garden only appears destroyed, but the seeds are still there! Soon it will be harvest time, and the seeds of perfect beauty will soon spring forth again!" he said. "You mean, I don't have to start over?" I said. "*No*, my child, your garden was never ruined, as long as you have good seeds, harvest time will surely come back again!"

I hope you will learn that the tragedies of this life are often unexpected. No matter what happens, one must indeed remember that harvest time will come again. You can start over. My garden was my body. It was indeed invaded by an uninvited guest. You may have a different garden in your life: it could be sickness, trials, or challenges. Let us not see our gardens as being ruined; let's search for the seeds. Water whatever you have left, and your flowers will surely spring forth again!

The Book of My Life

God created and then read the book of my life.

Page after page he read with great satisfaction.

Page one: I was sent to earth to change people and destructive ideas.

Page five: I was old enough to know right from wrong.

Page nine: I could discern the good of humankind from the evils.

When God turned to page twenty,

I had embraced multiple seasons of change.

By page twenty-five, I had fallen madly and completely in love.

A man loved me and gave me his prized possession.

By the end of the book, it was clear that I had come to one conclusion:

God was good.

He turned the page one final time:

God inhaled, and then I died.

I died loved and fulfilled.

God smiled and sighed after reading the book of my life.

He set the book on his golden bookshelf,

And then picked up his pen and began to create.

He created volume 2, which was the legacy that I left behind.

You are our Mothers

You are the first woman we ever met.
You are the only parent who cannot deny that the baby is yours.
To the only one who is a sister, daughter,
and mother all at the same time,
To the one who usually takes off her job for a sick child,
To the one who puts extra bubbles in the
bath water when a child is sick,
To the only one who is expected to cook, clean, wipe runny
noses, work a job, And love her man all on the same day,
You are our mothers.
You are the ones who have usually fought
for preaching God's Word.
You are the ones who have to teach when
you know you are called to preach.
You are the ones who have to teach Sunday school when you
should be leading the church. Oh, to be born a female!
You are our mothers.
To the ones who try to balance their demanding
schedules without any losses,
To the ones who usually have to choose their families over
working extra hours at work, you are our mothers.
To the ones who are their children's first
real teachers and counselors,
To the ones who are their husbands'
second mothers and best friends,
You are our mothers.
We love you, mothers, and we appreciate all the things that you do.
Without you, our haircuts would look terrible,
Our ponytails would be nappy and lopsided,
Our faces would be dirty, our noses would be runny,

Our clothes would be filthy. You are the most interesting women
we have ever Known. You are our mothers, and you are the
only ones who can never deny That we are your children.
No matter how far we go
Or how many times we trip and fall,
You will never deny that we are your children.
You are our mothers.